photography

First Edition

Lithographed in U.S.A.

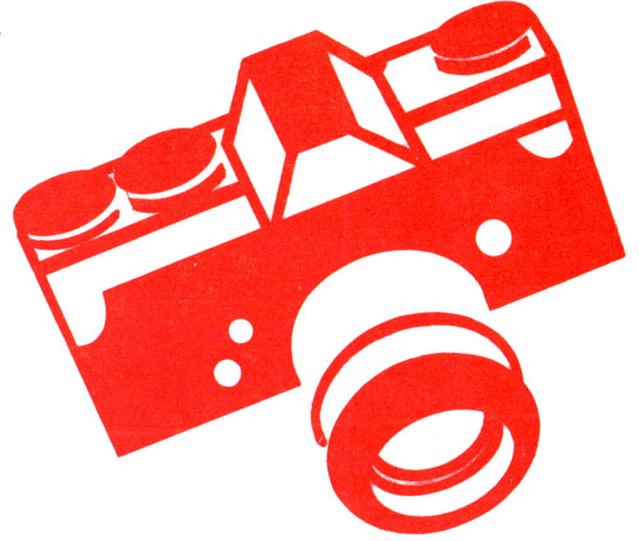

DR. WILBUR R. MILLER
University of Missouri — Columbia
Columbia, Missouri

DR. MARION E. MADDOX
University of Arkansas
Fayetteville, Arkansas

LAVON B. SMITH
Fayetteville, Arkansas

ROBERT A. McCOY
Hendersonville, North Carolina

DONALD GORE
Normal Community High School
Normal, Illinois

Reviewed by:

RICHARD J. BROEKHUIZEN
Nova High School
Ft. Lauderdale, Florida

basic industrial arts

Copyright © 1978

McKNIGHT Publishing Company
Bloomington, Illinois

**Library of Congress
Card Catalog Number: 78-53393**

SBN: 87345-789-7 Paperback
SBN: 87345-797-8 Hardbound

TABLE OF CONTENTS

Chapter 1

INTRODUCTION TO PHOTOGRAPHY

Photography is one of the most popular hobbies in the world. Also, many people make it their career, Figs. 1-1 and 1-2. Photography is both an art and a science. It invites creativity, yet it has certain laws. In this course you will learn to use a camera, develop film, and make prints. What you learn may spark your interest in photography as a hobby and may someday lead to a career.

THE IMPORTANCE OF PHOTOGRAPHY

The first picture was taken about 1826. At that time it took eight hours to take a picture. Today, a picture can be taken in 1/1000th of a second. It can be transmitted through wires and sent around the world in a matter of minutes. Pictures of an event that happens on the other side of the world can be seen hours later in newspapers or on television, Fig. 1-3. Just 10 years ago this would not have been possible. Photography appearing in newspapers, magazines, books, or television touches almost everyone's life every day.

News and entertainment are not the only ways that photography affects your life. Have

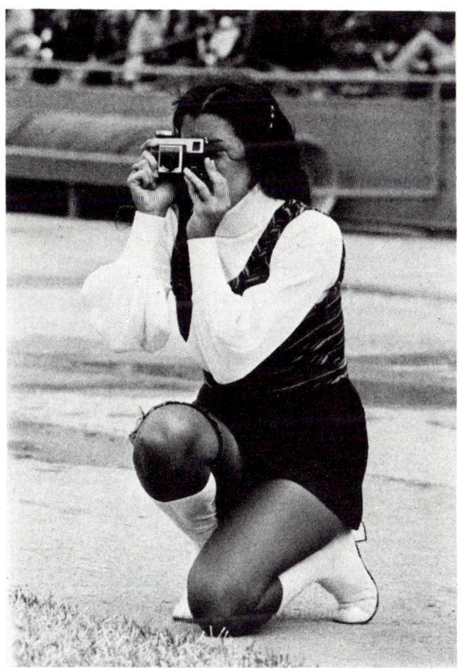

Fig. 1-1. A cheerleader at a football game finds a good subject for a snapshot. Many people make photography their hobby

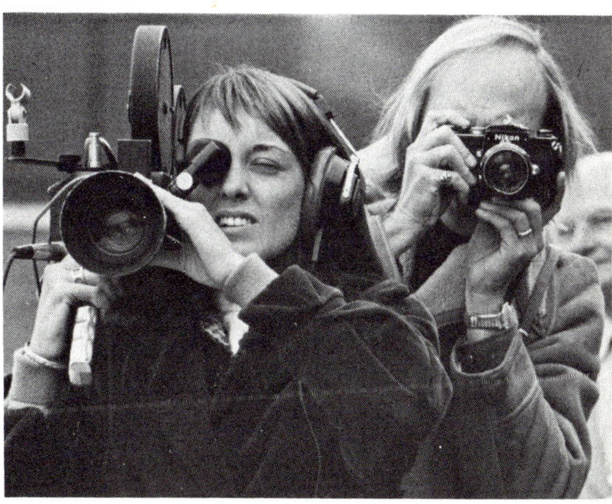

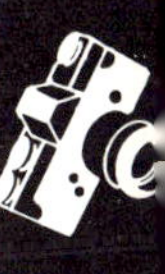

Fig. 1-2. Taking pictures is serious business to these people. They may have started as hobbyists, but now photography is their career.

you ever broken a bone? The X-rays that a doctor takes are a form of photography. Scientists who seek cures to illness use microscopes that have cameras in them. They can take pictures of virus which the unaided eye cannot see. Space explorers have transmitted pictures from the moon, Fig. 1-4. Millions of people take pictures of family, friends, and places as mementos of special times. Industry uses photography to inform and influence people, Fig. 1-5.

WHAT IS PHOTOGRAPHY?

Photography is the process of recording light on film. The subject photographed reflects light. The film, being sensitive to this light, records the subject. See Fig. 1-6.

Black and white photography involves four basic steps:

1. Taking the picture (exposing film to light).
2. Developing the film (making a negative).
3. Exposing photographic paper to make a print.

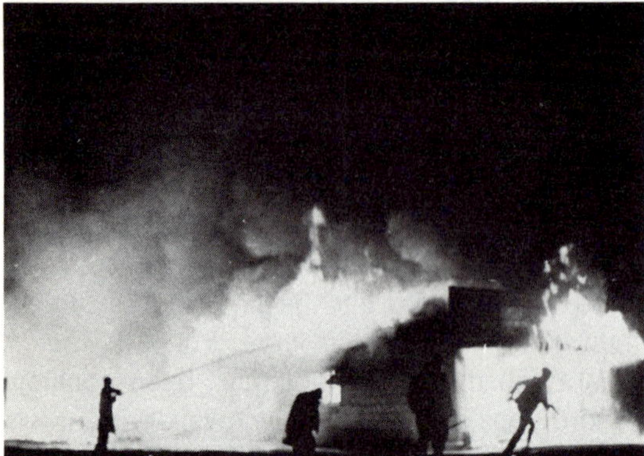

Fig. 1-3.   To keep the interest of their readers, newspapers want to use up-to-the-minute photographs.

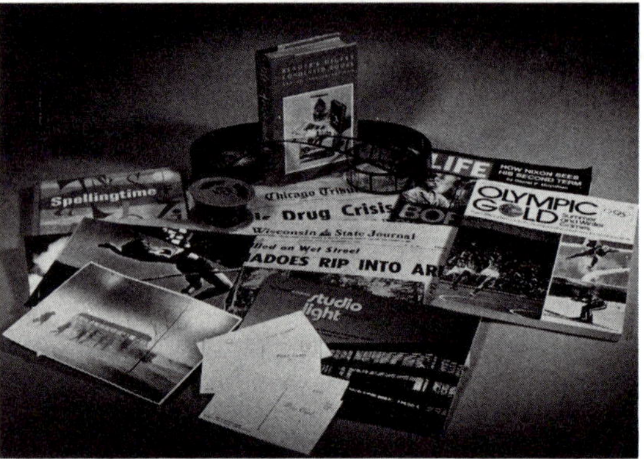

Fig. 1-5.   Photography has an influence on every activity and industry.

NASA National Aeronautics and Space Administration

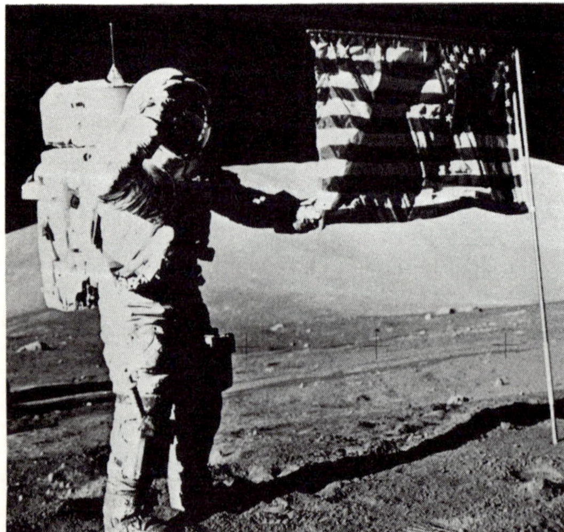

Fig. 1-4.   This picture was taken on the moon and transmitted back to earth within seconds.

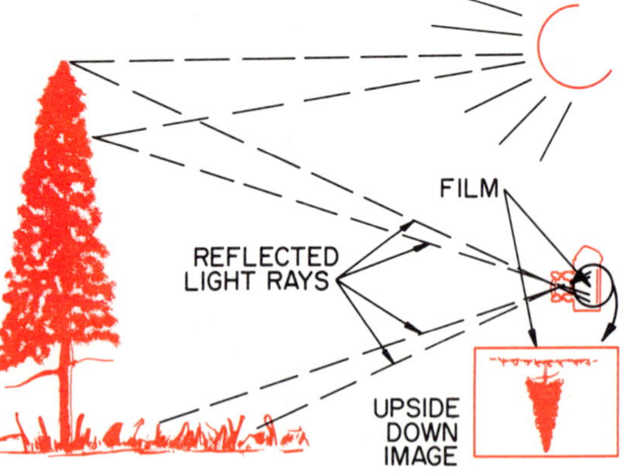

Fig. 1-6.   The subject reflects light rays. These light rays enter camera lens and strike the film. Silver halide crystals on the film change color according to how much light strikes them.

4. Developing the photographic paper.
Each step is shown in Fig. 1-7 and will be described in detail in later chapters.

TAKING THE PICTURE

Film is a thin, flexible material made up mainly of an **emulsion** which is adhered to a plastic base. See Fig. 1-8. Think of film as a thin surface with paint on it. The surface is the plastic base. The thin layer of paint represents the emulsion. The emulsion is composed of a gelatin that holds millions of **silver halide crystals.** These crystals are **sensitive to light.** When a picture is taken, light let into the camera strikes the crystals on the emulsion layer of the film

and records the image that the camera sees. To make the picture visible to the eye, the exposed film must be developed.

DEVELOPING THE FILM

Exposed film is taken out of the camera, removed from its protective cover, and placed in a **developer solution.** When film first comes out of the camera, it must be handled in complete darkness. Otherwise, the silver halide crystals would all be exposed to light and the picture would be lost. The developer solution turns the crystals that were exposed to light into black silver crystals. These black grains stay on the film. Next, the film is put in a **stop-bath**

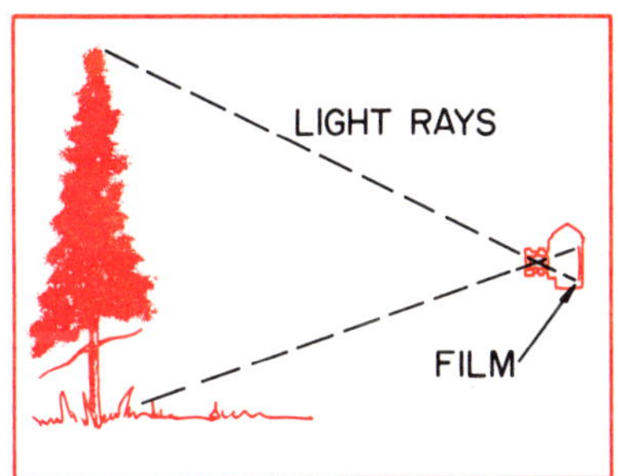

Step 1. Exposing the film. The camera lets light into the film. The image is recorded on the film emulsion.

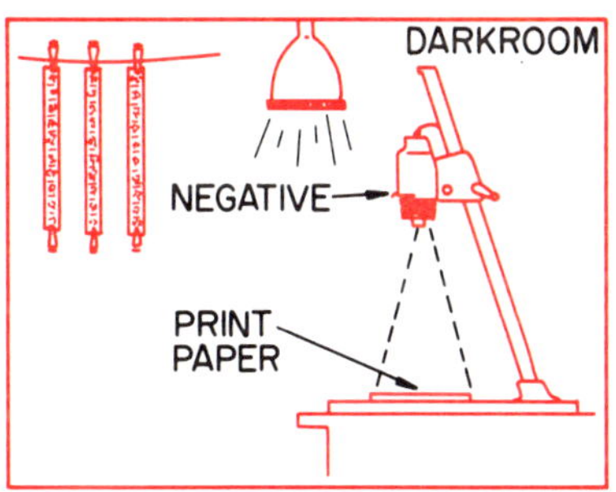

Step 3. Light is shined through the negative onto photographic paper.

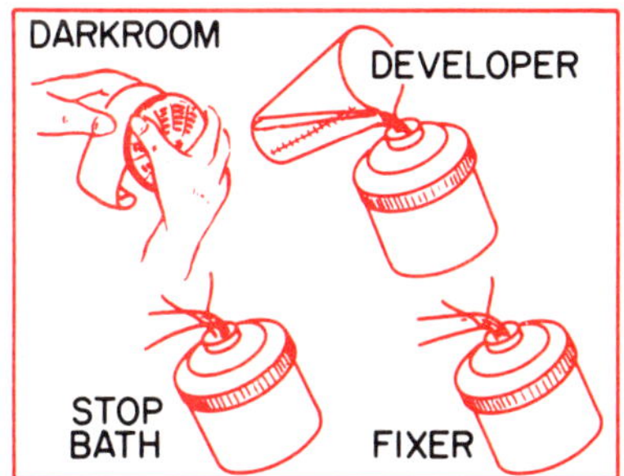

Step 2. The film is developed in a darkroom. Developed print film is called a negative.

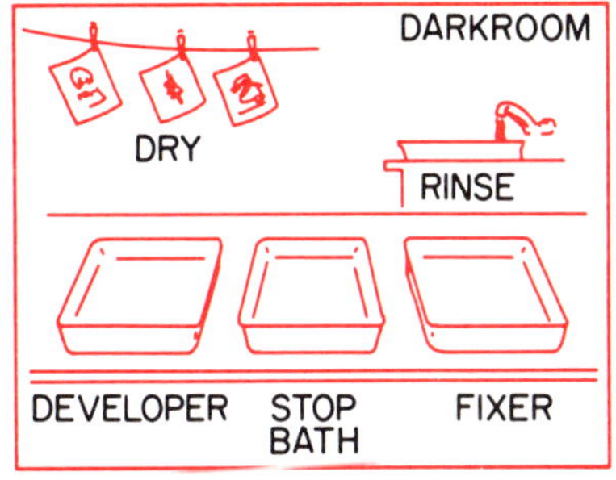

Step 4. The paper is developed to make a print.

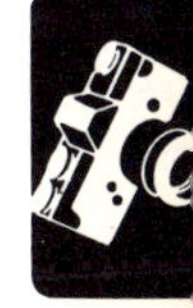

Fig. 1-7.   Photography involves 4 basic steps.

so that it does not overdevelop. The film then is put in a **fixer** solution. The fixer dissolves all of the undeveloped crystals that were not exposed· to the light. What is left of the original film is called a **negative.** See Fig. 1-9 The negative is then rinsed and allowed to dry.

Notice in Fig. 1-9 that a negative shows the image in reverse. That is, the black parts of the negative show the areas where the most silver halide crystals were exposed. It is in these areas that the most light struck the emulsion. The light parts of the negative show the areas where few halide crystals were exposed to light. All other areas are in shades of gray, depending upon the amount of light each area received when the picture was taken.

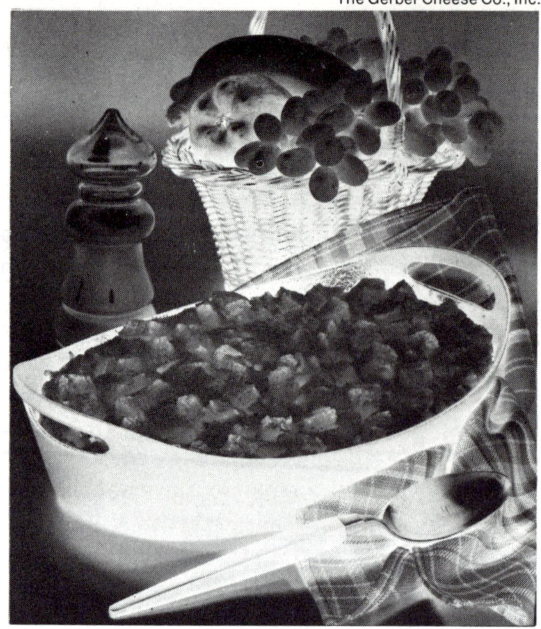

The Gerber Cheese Co., Inc.

A. Negative

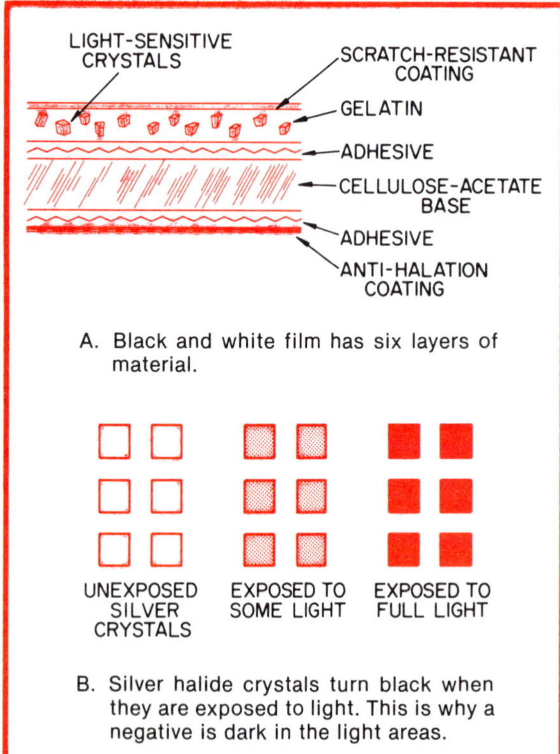

A. Black and white film has six layers of material.

B. Silver halide crystals turn black when they are exposed to light. This is why a negative is dark in the light areas.

Fig. 1-8.   Film Layers

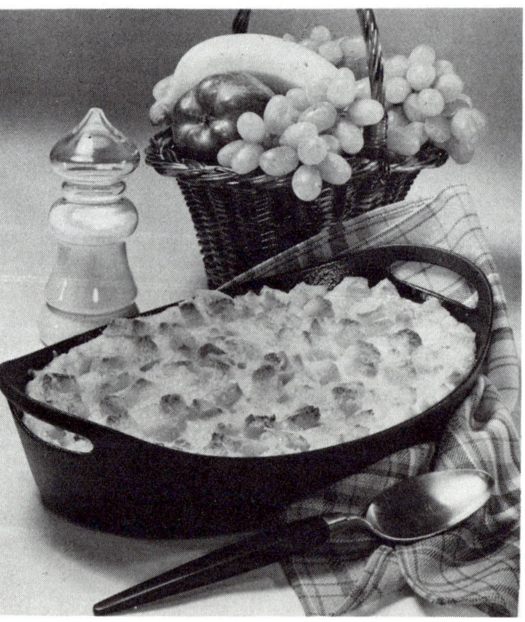

B. Print

Fig. 1-9.   In a negative the light and dark areas are reversed. When light is projected through the negative to make a print, the dark areas will not let light through. They will be light on the print.

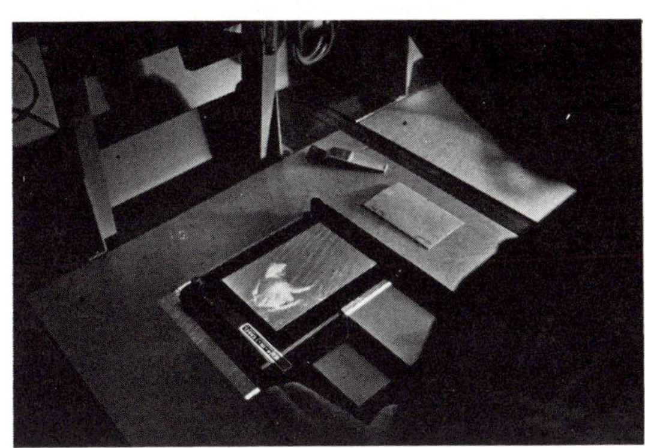

Step 1. Shine light through a negative onto photographic paper.

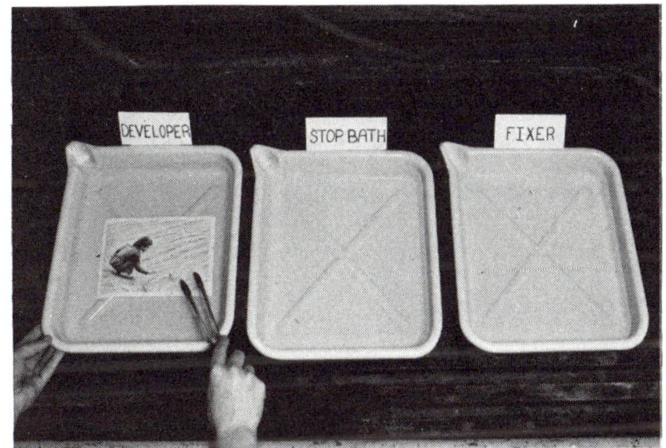

Step 2. Develop the photographic paper.

Fig. 1-10. Making a print.

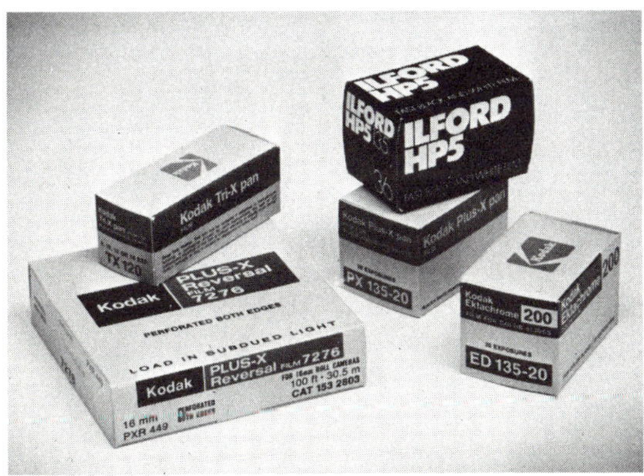

Fig. 1-11. Prints, slides, and movies are the three basic types of pictures. The film you choose depends upon the type of pictures you want and the size of your camera.

MAKING A PRINT

A positive print is made from the negative. A print is made by projecting light through the negative onto photographic paper that is coated with light-sensitive silver. In areas where the negative is dark, less light gets through to the paper. These areas, therefore, remain light. However, light projected through the light areas of the negative show up dark on the paper. The image that was in reverse on the negative now becomes a positive print. The exposure of the negative onto the photographic paper is called **projection printing.**

After the paper is exposed, it must be processed so the picture can be seen, Fig. 1-10. The same steps are used to process the photographic paper as were used to process the negatives.

1. Developer solution.
2. Stop bath.
3. Fixer.
4. Rinse.
5. Dry.

The negative can be used over and over again to make prints. It must be handled carefully, however, since scratches in the negative will show up on the prints.

Color film works the same way as black and white, except there are many layers of emulsion. Each layer records a different color. Also, different chemicals are used.

TYPES OF PICTURES

There are many types of pictures, but **prints, slides,** and **movies** are the most common, Fig. 1-11. Prints can be black and white or color pictures. Slides are pictures on processed film. Although they look somewhat like a negative the colors are not reversed. Slides are called **positive color transparencies.** Each transparency is framed in cardboard and usually is inserted in a projector for viewing. Prints

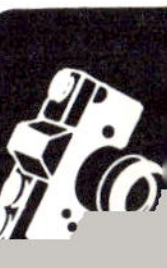

can be made from slides as well as from negatives. Movies are like slides, except that all the frames are left fastened together in a strip.

A movie camera is used to make movies. Still cameras are used to make prints and slides. Each requires different types of film. Film is made to serve many different purposes, Fig. 1-11. In later chapters, you will learn how to choose film.

The activities in this text are designed for use with a camera having adjustments for shutter speed, focal distance, and aperture. These features may be found on most 35 mm, 120 mm, and 220 mm cameras. If you do not have one of these cameras, you can still complete most of the activities with an inexpensive instamatic camera. These currently popular, cartridge-type cameras come in two sizes: 110 mm and 126 mm. The film in the 126 mm camera is comparable in width to that of the 35 mm film.

STUDY QUESTIONS

1. What is film?
2. What are the five steps in making a print?
3. What makes the silver halide crystals turn to black silver crystals?
4. Explain why a negative is reversed — that is, the dark areas are light and the light areas dark.
5. How is a print made from a negative?
6. What are three most common types of pictures?

ACTIVITY 1 — INTRODUCTION TO THE PHOTOGRAPHY LAB

Your teacher will show you the laboratory in which developing and printing are done. As you are introduced to the different kinds of equipment, remember that you should learn how to use them with care and caution.

Chapter **2**

MAKING PICTURES WITHOUT A CAMERA

Shadow pictures can be made without the use of a camera, Fig. 2-1. They are called **photograms.** They are made by placing objects on photographic paper and exposing the paper to light. By making a photogram, you will learn some basic principles of photography. Also, you will learn how to use the enlarger and how to process prints. With a little practice you will be able to process prints of pictures you have taken.

THE DARKROOM

Film is processed in a darkroom. Any room can be used as a darkroom as long as it can be made **completely** dark. Total darkness protects the silver halide crystals until they are developed. Red safelights are used during some of the film processing.

The darkroom is used for three basic processes:

1. To develop film.
2. To make contact prints (pictures the same size as the negatives).
3. To make enlargements (pictures larger than the negatives).

The procedures for all three processes are similar and require the same basic steps. After exposure of the print paper, it is processed in the following sequence:

1. Developer solution.
2. Stop bath.
3. Fixer.
4. Rinse.
5. Dry.

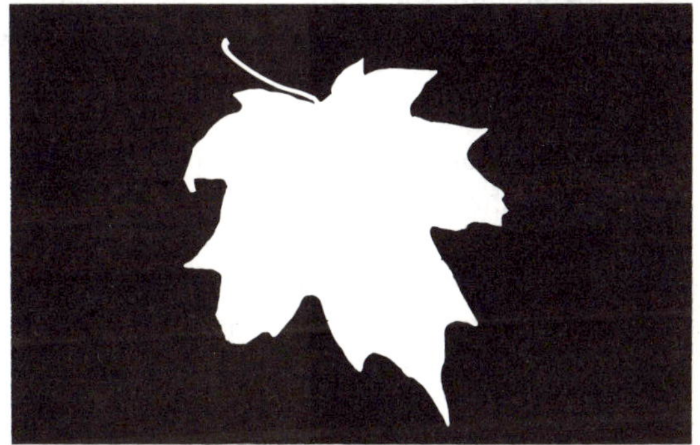

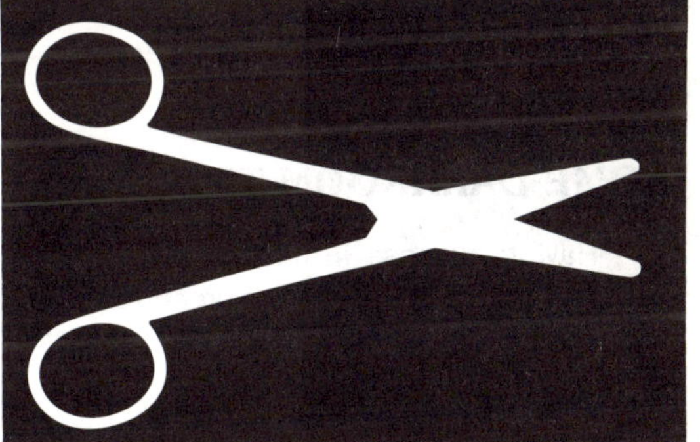

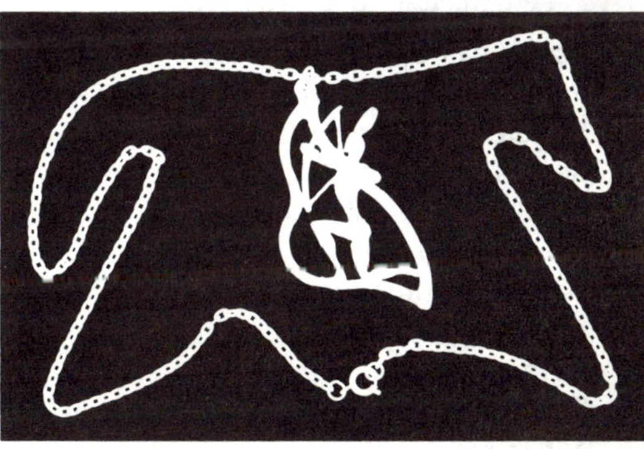

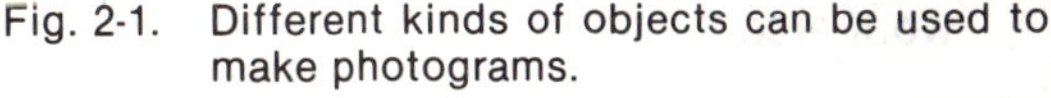

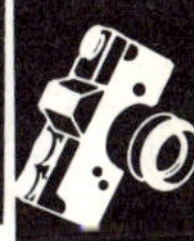

Fig. 2-1. Different kinds of objects can be used to make photograms.

Exposure to light. Film is exposed to light that enters the camera as the picture is taken. Contact prints which are the same size as the film and enlargements are made by projecting light through the negatives onto photographic paper. See. Fig. 2-2. Just as film must be exposed in the camera, photographic paper must be exposed to light in the darkroom. Developing film will be covered in a later chapter. Here, you will learn how to develop photographic paper.

Developing solution. After the paper has been exposed to light, it is put in a **developing solution,** Fig. 2-3. The silver crystals that were exposed to light will turn different densities of black. The longer the paper is left in the developer, the blacker the crystals get.

Stop bath. Next, the paper is put in a stop bath. This stops the developer so the print does not get too dark. The stop bath neutralizes the action of the developer.

Fixer. The print is then placed in a fixer bath. The fixer removes undeveloped and unexposed crystals.

Rinsing and drying. The print is rinsed in water and allowed to **dry.**

SOME DARKROOM TIPS

Having success in making prints will depend on how well you follow procedures. Here are some hints to help you get good prints.

1. Always read directions carefully.
2. Avoid transferring excess developer into the stop bath tray. If an indicator stop bath is used, it will appear clear under the darkroom light. It turns dark when no longer effective.
3. Handle the prints with tongs, not your fingers. Touch only the outside border of the print. Use separate tongs for the developing solution and the stop bath.
4. While the prints are in the solutions, agitate them gently. Carefully rock the tray back and forth.
5. Be neat. Make sure **none of the chemicals get mixed together.** Do not leave a messy work area.

ACTIVITY 2 — MAKING A PHOTOGRAM

You can use almost any object to make a photogram. Leaves, small tools, cutouts, string, or even a kitchen strainer make interesting photograms. You are limited only by your imagination.

You will use the enlarger to make your photogram. Fig. 2-4 shows the main parts of the

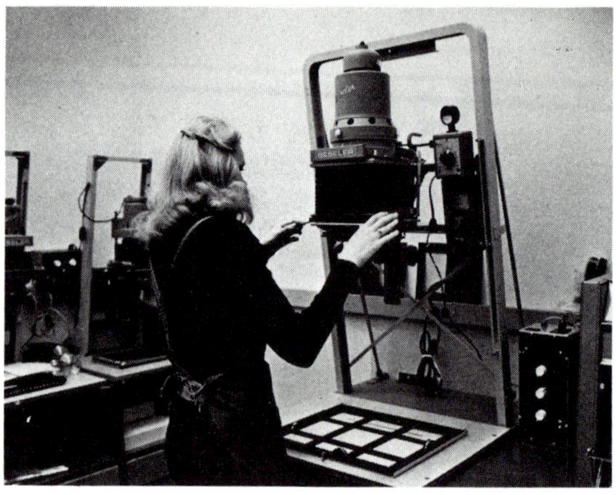

Fig. 2-2.   Prints are made by projecting light through a negative onto photographic paper. Here, a photographer uses an enlarger to make a print.

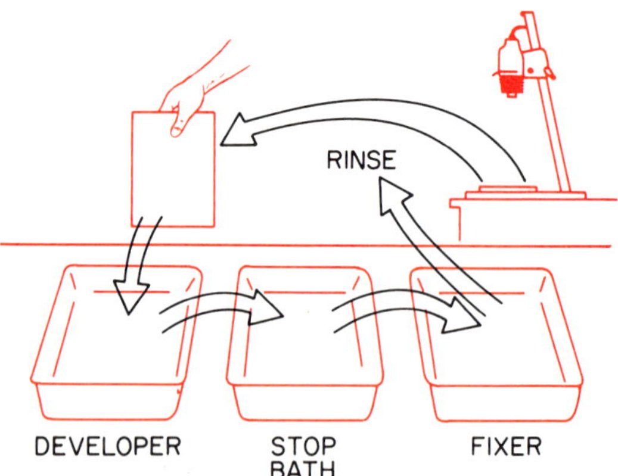

Fig. 2-3.   After photographic paper is exposed to light, the same three steps are used to develop the image on the paper as are used to develop film.

enlarger. Your teacher will demonstrate the enlarger you will use.

Materials Needed

Objects for the image
Polycontrast[F] paper* 5 x 7 in.
Dektol® developer
Acetic acid stop bath
Fixing solution

Hypo clear
Pakasol® solution to prevent spotting (if desired)
5 trays
Enlarger

*Note: If resin coated paper is used, the hypo clear and Pakasol® solutions are not needed.

Preparing the Chemicals

If your teacher has not already done so, mix the chemicals, following these directions. Or mix according to labels on the bottles.

Tray 1: **Developer.** Mix 16 oz. (473 ml) of Dektol with 32 oz. (946 ml) of water. (This is called a 1:2 ratio)

Tray 2: **Stop Bath:** Mix 1-1/2 oz. (44 ml) of acetic acid with 32 oz. (946 ml) of water. An indicator stop bath can be prepared by mixing 2 oz. of concentrate per gallon of water or 16 ml per liter.

Tray 3: **Fixer.** Mix 16 oz. (473 ml) stock fixer with 16 oz. (473 ml) of water.

Tray 4: **Fixer clear** (hypo clear). Use 16 oz. (473 ml) straight hypo clear solution. The hypo clears the fixer away faster so that you do not have to rinse as long.

Exposing the Photogram

1. Prepare the enlarger:
   a. Check to see that it has a 50 mm lens.
   b. Raise the enlarger head until its light pattern, when focused, just covers the glass plate area. Turn off the light.
   c. Close the aperture and then open two clicks. Ask your teacher for help.
2. Turn off the main lights and turn on the safelight.
3. Place a 5 x 7 in. piece of polycontrast F paper in the easel. Arrange the objects on the paper in the desired pattern. Turn on the enlarger light.
4. Expose for about 12 seconds.

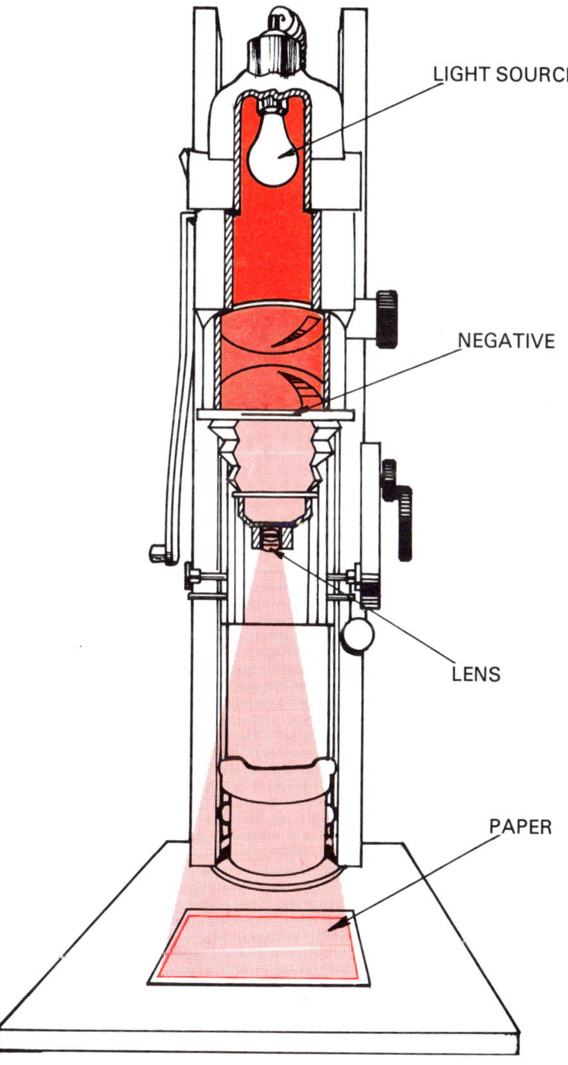

Fig. 2-4.   Enlarger

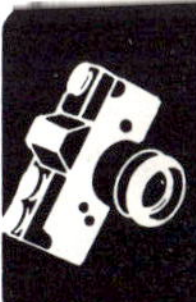

Developing the Print

1. Use tongs to pick up the print and place it face up in the developer. Be sure all the print is in the solution. In 15 or 20 seconds an image should appear. If the image appears in less time, the paper has been exposed to too much light for a good print. Gently rock the tray so that the developer moves around. Allow development to continue until the desired contrast between black and white has been reached. With an ideal exposure, this may require up to 1-1/2 minutes, Fig. 2-5.

2. Remove the print from the developer and let it drip for a few seconds. Place it in the stop bath, using the stop bath tongs. **Do not use the developer tongs.** Be sure the print is completely covered. Leave it in the stop bath for 15 seconds.

3. Remove the print from the stop bath and let it drip for a few seconds. Use the fixer tongs to put it in the fixing solution for 8-10 minutes. Agitate once every 30 seconds.

4. Remove the print from the fix and let it drip for several seconds. Place the print in the hypo clear for 2 to 4 minutes.

5. Remove the print and put it in an empty tray. Put the tray in the sink and let water **slowly** run into the tray for 5-10 minutes. This is called **rinsing the print.**

6. Remove the print from the rinse and place it in the Pakasol solution for 5 minutes.

7. Remove the print and let it dry. Your teacher will show you the procedure for drying the print.

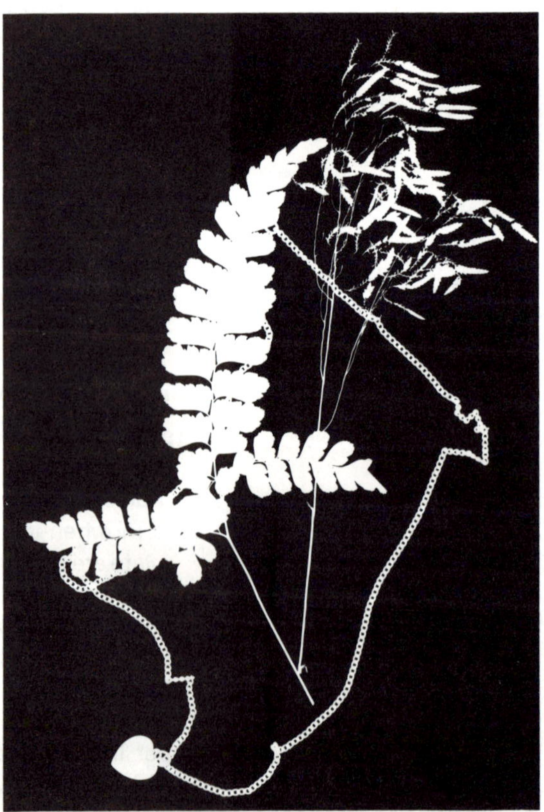

Fig. 2-5.   Develop the print until there is good contrast between black and white.

<table>
<tr><td>Chapter 3</td><td style="text-align:right"><h1>THE CAMERA</h1></td></tr>
</table>

There are many different types of cameras, Fig. 3-1. Some are simple to use because they are totally automatic. All the photographer has to do is aim and snap the picture. In most cases, the resulting picture turns out well. Other cameras are complex. Several adjustments must be made. Decisions must be made regarding the amount of light allowed to enter the camera and the speed at which the picture will be taken. Such cameras are for those persons who pursue photography as a career or serious hobby. This course will teach you how to make these adjustments.

All cameras have the same basic parts. You should know these parts and their function. Study Figs. 3-2 and 3-3 carefully.

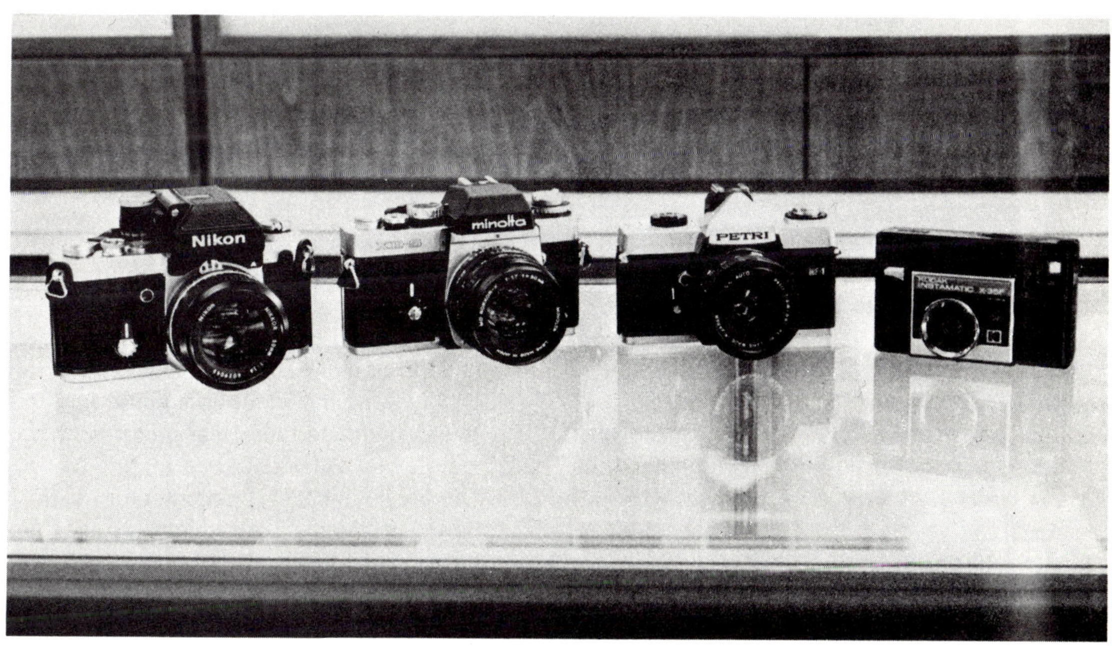

Fig. 3-1. Some cameras are simple to use. Others require a good knowledge of photography. The best type of camera for you depends upon your needs.

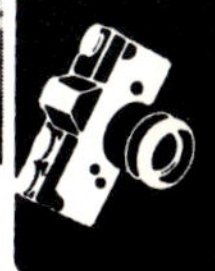

Fig.3-2

THE PARTS OF A CAMERA

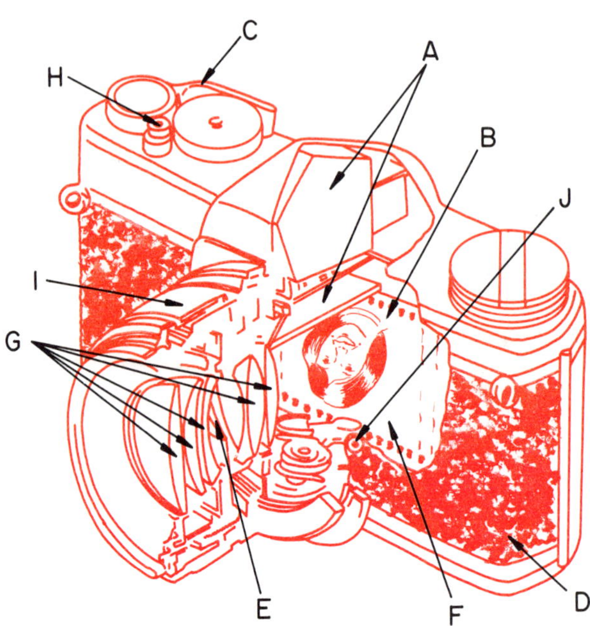

A. **The viewing system** shows what the camera sees. It lets the photographer see the subject.

B. **The film** receives the reflected light from the subject being photographed. It records the picture on its light sensitive surface of the film in the camera.

C. **The film advance** system winds the film from one spool to another. It moves the film forward each time a picture is taken so two pictures are not exposed on the same piece of film.

D. **The camera body** contains all the parts. The body protects the film from all light except that which enters when the picture is taken.

E. **The diaphragm** controls the amount of light reaching the film. The diaphragm has a hole in it that is adjustable to let more or less light into the camera.

F. **The shutter** is the second light control device. It lets no light reach the film except when the picture is taken. The shutter controls the amount of time allowed for light to reach the film.

G. **The lens** focuses the light rays from the subject and makes a reversed, upside down image on the film.

H. **The shutter release button** is pushed by the photographer to open the shutter. This allows light to enter the camera.

I. **The focusing control** moves the lens back or forth to make a sharp image on the film. In this way, the focus is adjusted so that the camera can take clear pictures of subjects close or far away.

J. **The flash socket** is the plug-in for the flash unit. The flash provides light so that pictures can be taken in a low level light, such as indoors or at night.

After the picture is taken, the photographer advances the film and the camera is ready to take the next picture.

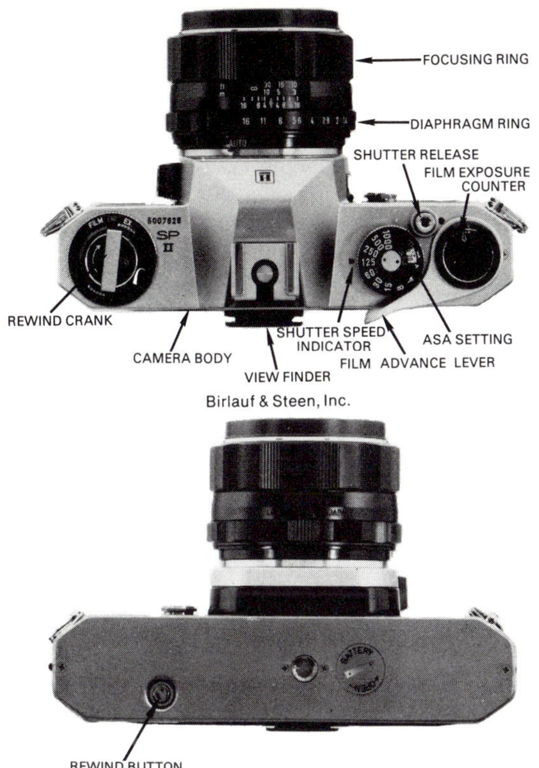

Fig. 3-3.   Outside parts of a 35 mm camera.

HOW A CAMERA WORKS

When a picture is taken, it sets up a chain of action. The photographer pushes the shutter release button to take the picture. When the shutter opens, the light rays coming through the lens and diaphragm are projected onto the film. The lens redirects the rays to make the image small enough to fit on the film. Also, the lens turns the image upside down, Fig. 3-4. The diaphragm controls the number of light rays that reach the film. On a sunny, bright day, few rays are needed for a good picture. Therefore, the hole made when the diaphragm opens should be small. This hole is referred to as the **aperture.** On a cloudy day or indoors, more light is needed. The aperture of the diaphragm should be bigger to let lots of rays reach the film. After the shutter opens to let in the light, it quickly closes again. If the shutter is allowed to remain open too long, the film is exposed to too much light. The image on the negative will be dark. This results in a picture that is too light and faded. The film is **overexposed.** The picture it produces on print paper appears **underexposed. Underexposed** film occurs when the shutter is not open long enough. The negative is very light. When used to expose print paper it produces a dark picture, Fig. 3-5.

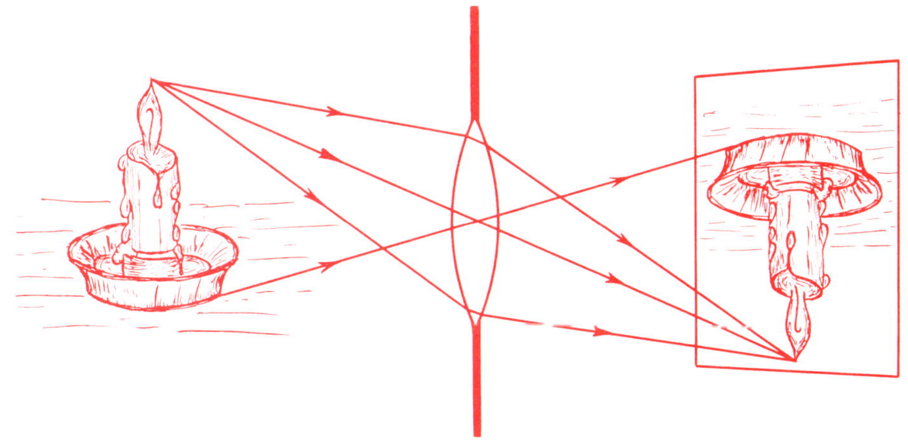

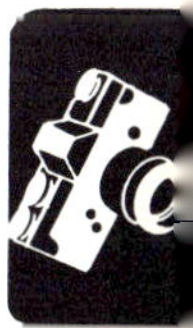

Fig. 3-4.   The camera lens reorganizes the light rays and focuses them on the film. The lens reverses the image, turning it upside down.

	Negative	Print
Shutter Open Too Long	**Overexposed.** The negative is too dark.	**Underexposed.** The negative does not allow enough light to pass through for correct exposure of the print paper. Print very light or "weak."
Shutter Not Open Long Enough	**Underexposed.** The negative is too light.	**Overexposed.** The negative allows too much light to pass through for correct exposure of print paper. Print very dark and faded.
Shutter Open Correct Length Of Time	**Correctly Exposed.** The negative has good contrast.	**Correctly Exposed.** The print has true contrast of black and white.

Fig. 3-5.   The amount of light reaching the film determines the exposure required.

STUDY QUESTIONS

1. What is the purpose of the viewing system?
2. What two parts of a camera are light control devices?
3. What is the purpose of the diaphragm?
4. What is the hole in the diaphragm called? Explain how the size of the hole is changed in reference to the light available.
5. What is the purpose of the shutter?
6. What part of the camera reorganizes the light rays so they make a focused image on the film?

ACTIVITY 3 — MAKING A PINHOLE CAMERA

Making and using your own pinhole camera helps you learn the basics about cameras. Also, you will have fun taking pictures with a camera you have made yourself, Fig. 3-6.

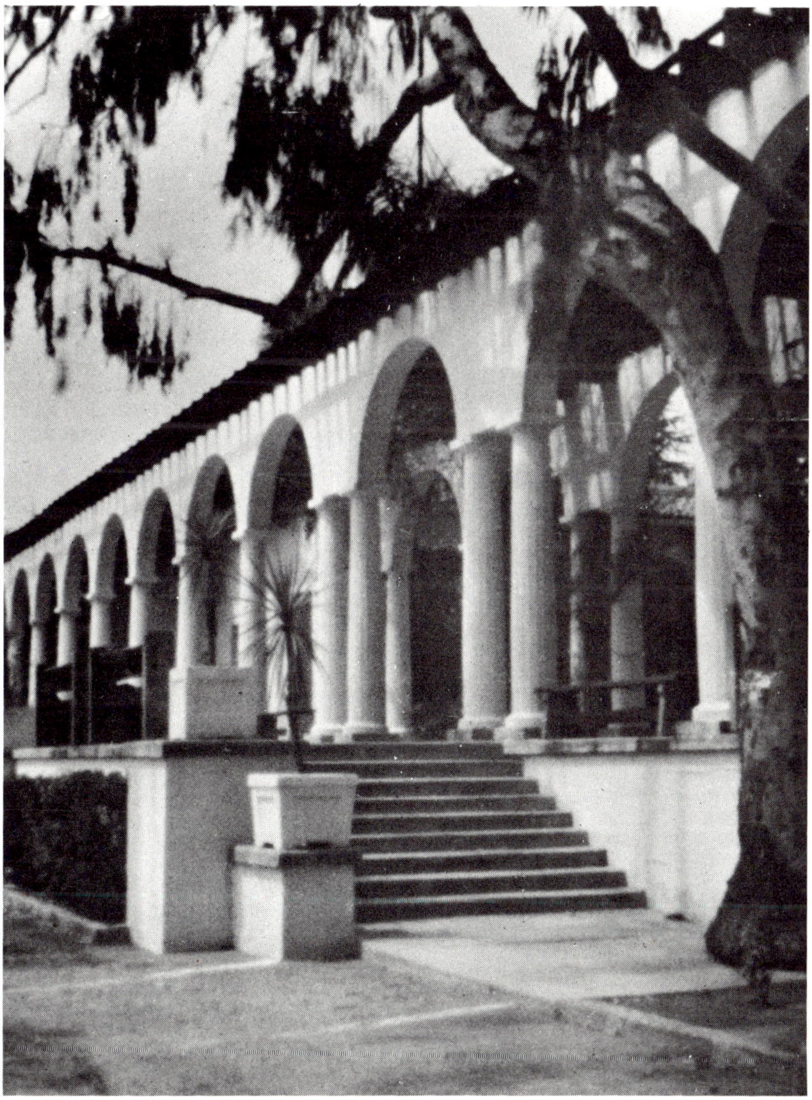

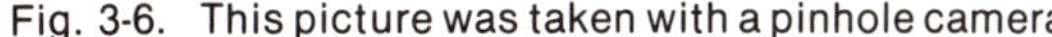

Fig. 3-6. This picture was taken with a pinhole camera.

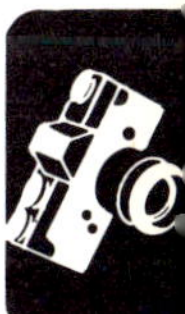

You can make a pinhole camera from materials found at home or in the shop, Fig. 3-7.

Materials Needed

Shoebox or similar box, 2 or 3 lb. coffee can, peanut can, or round oatmeal carton
Small piece of heavy duty aluminum foil
2 index cards or small flat piece of styrofoam
1 small piece of black paper about 1 inch (25.5 mm) by 1-1/2 inch (38 mm) in size
Tape, electrical or masking
Dull, black paint
#10 sewing needle or a straight pin
1 sheet of film or print paper
Plus-X Pan film 4147 ASA 125 (4″ x 5″) or Tri-X Pan 4147 professional ASA 320
Ortho Film Type 3 2556 (4″ x 5″)
Polycontrast F print paper either single or medium weight

Directions

1. Choose a box or can for the camera body. Your teacher may have a Kodak booklet showing how to make a pinhole camera from a 126 mm film cartridge.
2. Cut a 1 inch (25.5 mm) hole in one end or side. If your can or box opens on one end only, cut the hole in the end that **does not open.**

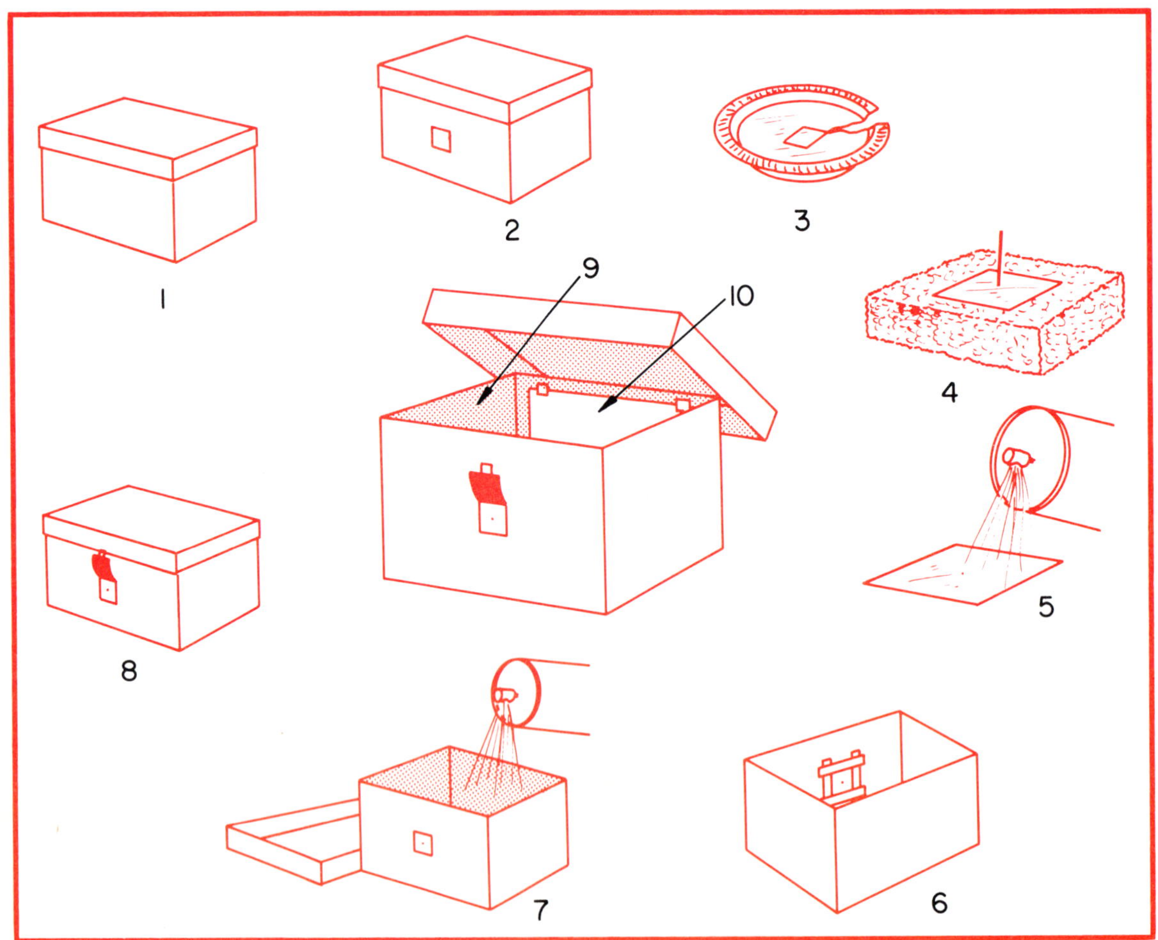

Fig. 3-7.   A pinhole camera is easy to make and use. Be sure your camera allows no light to enter.

3. Cut a piece of heavy duty aluminum foil larger than the hole you just cut. Aluminum foil from a disposable pie pan produces best results. Do not let the foil get wrinkled.

4. Place the foil between two index cards or on a piece of styrofoam. Push a #10 sewing needle or a common straight pin through the foil to a point halfway up the needle shank. Rotate (turn) the needle as you push it in and pull it out. Do not make the hole too big. Future pinhole cameras could be constructed with different sized pinholes to determine best results.

5. Remove the needle. Blacken one side of the foil with a candle flame or spray with dull, black paint. If the hole becomes blocked, use the needle to carefully reopen it.

6. Tape the foil on the inside of the camera, centering the pinhole over the one-inch hole. The blackened side of the foil must face the inside of the camera. Tape all four sides of the foil.

7. Paint the entire inside of your camera with a dull black paint, avoiding the foil. If you use a coffee can with a plastic lid, paint the inside of the lid. Cover the outside of the lid with aluminum foil after the camera is loaded with film or print paper.

8. Tape a small piece of black paper on the outside of the camera so it covers the pinhole. Tape along the top edge only. Use a small piece of tape at the bottom to hold the paper "shutter" down between exposures.

9. Look through your camera from the inside to make sure no light is coming in through the covered pinhole.

10. Now, load the camera. If Plus-X or Tri-X Pan sheet film is used, all loading, unloading, and processing must be done in **total darkness.** If print paper or sheets of ortho film are used, loading, unloading, and processing can be done under a standard darkroom safelight. The size of film or print paper can vary with the construction of your camera.

Tape the film or paper to the inside back of the camera with the emulsion side toward the pinhole. You can tell the emulsion side of Plus-X Pan film by feeling the notches on the film. When you turn the film so the notches are on the upper right-hand corner, the emulsion side is facing you, Fig. 3-8. The polycontrast F paper emulsion side is shiny under the safelight. Ortho film has a light side and dark side. The light side of the film is the emulsion side. Before leav-

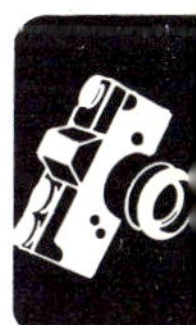

Fig. 3-8.   When loading your pinhole camera, be sure the emulsion side is facing the pinhole. The notches will be on the right hand side as you hold the film.

ing the darkroom, close the camera securely. Be sure the pinhole is covered.

11. Now you are ready to take the picture. Choose a subject that will remain perfectly still, such as a parked car, building, or landscape. Your camera must be laid on or taped to a solid surface such as a table or chair. **Do not hold it in your hands when you take the picture.**

12. Choose your exposure time from the chart, Fig. 3-9. Count carefully or use the second hand on a watch to expose the film the correct amount of time. When you are ready to take the picture, open the pinhole cover. Leave it open for the correct amount of time. Do not jiggle the camera. When time is up, close the pinhole.

13. **Leave the film in the camera** until you are ready to develop it. You will learn how to develop the film or print paper in the next chapter.

	LIGHTING CONDITIONS	
	Bright hazy, sun, snow	Bright cloudy, or open shade
Tri-X Film 4147 ASA 320	1 to 2 seconds	4 to 8 seconds
Plus-X Film 4147 ASA 125	3 to 5 seconds	9 to 17 seconds
Ortho Film 2556 Type 3	10 seconds	15 seconds
Polycontrast F Print Paper	20 seconds	25 seconds

Fig. 3-9.   Exposure Times

Chapter 4   DEVELOPING SHEET FILM

You learned the five steps of developing when you made your photogram. In review, these five steps are:

1. Developer solution.
2. Stop Bath.
3. Fixer.
4. Rinse.
5. Dry.

Film also goes through these five steps to make a negative. In this lesson, you will develop the film you took with your pinhole camera.

Most film must be developed in **total darkness.** Even the smallest amount of light will ruin it. Ortho films and print can be handled under a standard darkroom safelight without being exposed.

The temperature of the developer is also important. The ideal temperature is 68° (20° C). It is not always possible that the developer will have this temperature. If it does not, you must adjust the amount of time that the film is in the developer. The **warmer** the developer, the **less time** the film should stay in the solution. The instructions on the developing solutions will tell you the amount of time to leave the film in the developing solution.

The best way to learn how to develop film is to do it. Read the following instructions carefully and then develop the film used in your pinhole camera.

ACTIVITY 4
PART 1 — DEVELOPING THE FILM

Materials Needed

Developer for Plus- X or Tri-X film
Stop bath
Fixer
Hypo clear
Heavy black paper

1. Arrange the trays in the darkroom and mix the following chemicals according to directions.
   a. Tray 1: Developer
   b. Tray 2: Stop bath
   c. Tray 3: Fixer. Use full strength stock solution.
   d. Tray 4: Hypo clear. No mixing needed.
2. Check the temperature of the developer. Follow the chart in Fig. 4-1 to determine the amount of time needed to develop the film.
3. Set a timer for the amount of time your film should stay in the developer. The timer should not be started until the film is actually placed in the developer.

Temperature of Developer		Minutes in Developer
°F	°C	
67°	19.4°	6:00
68°	20.0°	5:45
69°	20.5°	5:30
70°	21.0°	5:15
71°	21.6°	5:00
72°	22.2°	4:40
73°	22.7°	4:30
74°	23.3°	4:15
75°	23.9°	4:05

Fig. 4-1.   Development times for Plus X film.

4. Read the remaining steps carefully so that you can perform them in the darkroom.
   a. Remove the film from the camera in total darkness.
   b. Place the film in the developer with the emulsion side up. At the same time, start the timer. Gently rock the developer tray for the entire time the film is in the developer.
   c. When the timer goes off, remove the film from the developer. Let it drip over the developer tray a few seconds and then place it in the stop bath for 30 seconds. Do **not** let any extra developer solution get into the stop bath.
   d. Remove the film from the stop bath and let it drip. Place it in the fixing solution for 5-10 minutes. After the first couple of minutes in the fixer you can turn on the lights.
   e. Remove the film from the fixer and let it drip for several seconds. Place it in the hypo clear solution for 30 seconds.
   f. Use an empty tray to wash the film for 5 minutes. Do not waste water.
   g. Hang the negative to dry.

NOTE: If ortho film or print paper are used to make the negative, develop as explained in Activity 2 — Making a Photogram.

PART 2 — MAKING A CONTACT PRINT

Making a contact print is similar to making a photogram. Follow these directions carefully.

1. Raise the enlarger head until its focused pattern covers the glass plate.
2. Turn off all lights except the safelight. Place the negative on top of a piece of photographic paper. The film must be emulsion side down (dull side) and the paper emulsion side up (shiny side).
3. Place the film and photographic paper on the baseboard of the enlarger. Cover with glass, Fig. 4-2. This procedure will be used

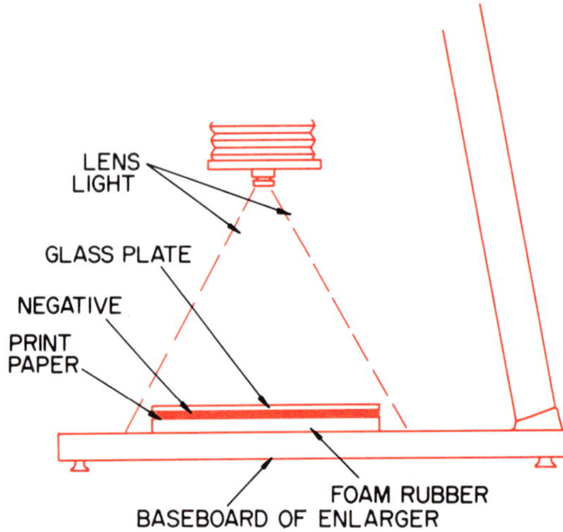

Fig. 4-2.   Making a contact print in the enlarger.

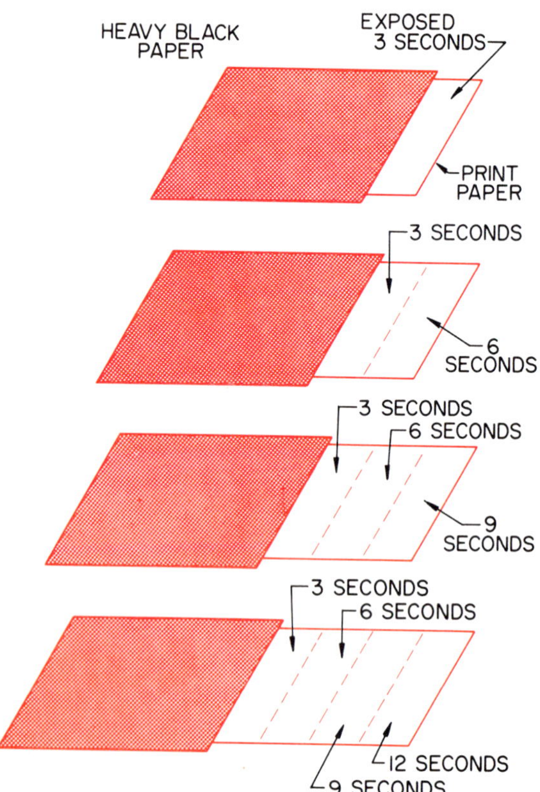

Fig. 4-3.   Test strip procedures.

for Tri-X, Plus-X, and Ortho films. If a paper negative is prepared, wet both the negative and a fresh piece of print paper. Place the unexposed paper on the piece of glass, emulsion side up. Place the paper negative face down against the unexposed print paper. Rub the two together to insure good contact and blot away the excess water.

4. Before you can make a final print, you must determine the amount of light needed. To do this, make a test strip, using four different exposures, Figs. 4-3 and 4-4. Follow this procedure to expose each test piece.

   a. Cover all but the **right-hand** 1/4 of the negative with heavy black paper. Turn the enlarger on for 3 seconds. Turn it off after 3 seconds.

   b. Uncover another 1/4 and turn on the enlarger and expose again for 3 seconds.

   c. Repeat this procedure two more times.

   d. Develop the test strip just as you did the photogram. Follow the directions on page 10 to develop your test strip.

5. Choose the best exposure from the test strip. Place your negative and a new piece of photographic paper on the enlarger as shown in Fig. 4-2.

6. Turn on the enlarger for the correct exposure time, as determined by the test strip.

7. Develop your print using the same procedure as used for your test strip.

8. Dry your print according to your teacher's instructions.

Seconds of Exposure			
1st				3
2nd			3	3
3rd		3	3	3
4th	3	3	3	3
Total Sec.	3	6	9	12

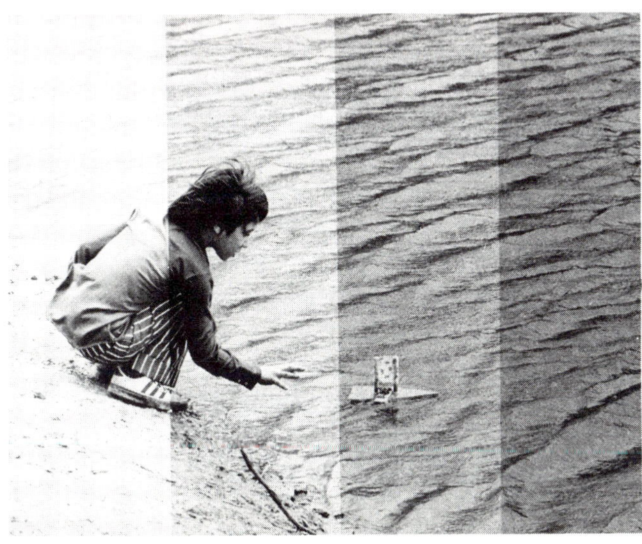

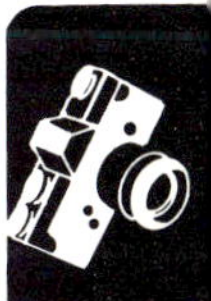

Fig. 4-4.   A test strip determines the proper exposure for the print. Notice that as you work from the right-hand side each section is exposed three more sections than the section to its left.

SHOOTING YOUR FIRST ROLL OF FILM

Chapter **5**

Before you shoot your first roll of film in a camera, you must learn how to do these things:

1. Load the film in the camera.
2. Set the aperture.
3. Set the shutter speed.
4. Focus.

Learning how to do each of these correctly will help you achieve good pictures.

LOADING THE CAMERA

Each camera loads differently. Your teacher will show you how to load the film in the camera you will be using. Also, each camera comes with an owner's manual that tells how to **use** the camera, Fig. 5-1. Before using any camera, read the manual carefully. Part of being a good photographer is knowing how to use your equipment.

Before loading the camera, check the film's **ASA rating.** ASA is a term that indicates how sensitive the film is to light. The **higher** the ASA, the **less light** the film needs to take a good picture. You will learn more about films and ASA ratings in a later chapter. Be sure the light meter of your camera is set for the proper ASA rating. Not all cameras have a built-in light meter that requires ASA adjustment. Ask your teacher if you are not sure about the camera you are using.

After the camera is loaded and closed, advance the film two frames. Most cameras have an automatic counter that tells you when you have reached the first unexposed frame. Unless you are using a cartridge, the first two pictures are not usable because they are exposed to light when the camera is loaded. As you advance the film, watch the rewind knob. If it turns, you know the film is winding. If it does not turn, ask you teacher for help. Instamatic cameras such as 110 mm and 126 mm models are more easily loaded. The cartridges are inserted. Once the camera is closed, the film is advanced until the number 1 appears in the counter window.

SETTING THE APERTURE

Remember that there are two factors that determine the amount of light reaching the film. One is the **aperture** which is the size of the hole in the diaphragm when it is opened. The other is the **shutter speed,** or how fast the picture is taken.

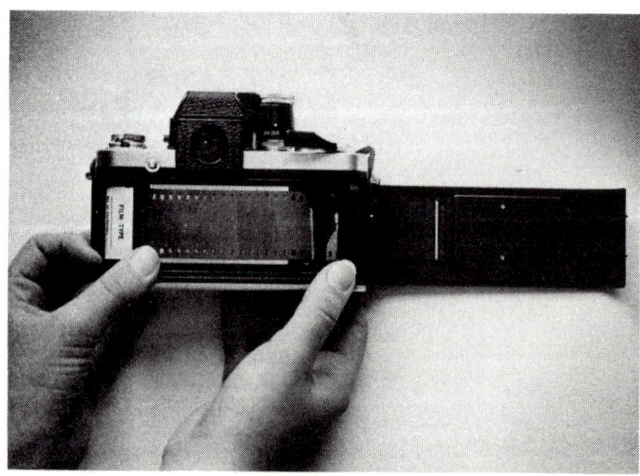

Fig. 5-1.   Know how to load the film properly in your camera. Always check the camera manual for correct procedure.

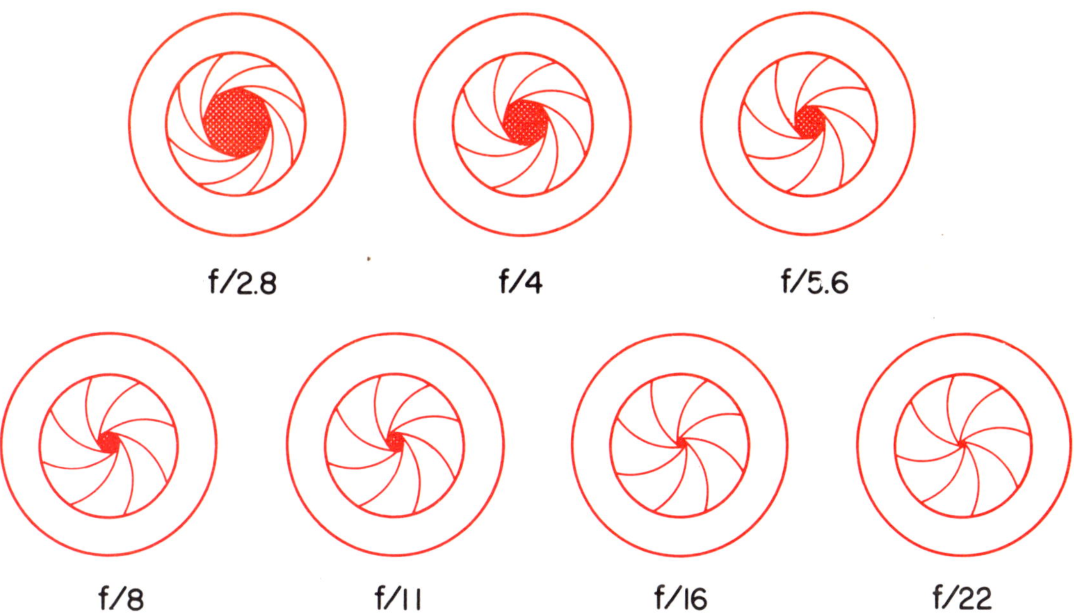

Fig. 5-2. The aperture controls the amount of light entering the camera. Notice that a setting of f/2.8 lets more light in than a setting of f/22.

The aperture is adjusted according to the amount of light available. On a bright day, the hole should be small. Otherwise, too much light would reach the film. On a dark, cloudy day, the hole should be large to let in more light. The size of the aperture is determined by f-stops. Figure 5-2 shows the f-stops on a 35 millimeter single lens reflex camera with a 50 mm lens. The f-stops vary on different lenses, but the most common ones are shown in Figs. 5-2 and 5-3. Notice that as the **f-stop number gets larger, the aperture gets smaller.** This is because f-stops are actually fractions. A setting of f/8 is 1/8th. A setting of f/11 is 1/11th. The 1/11th is a smaller fraction than 1/8th. Which setting lets in more light f/16 or f/2?

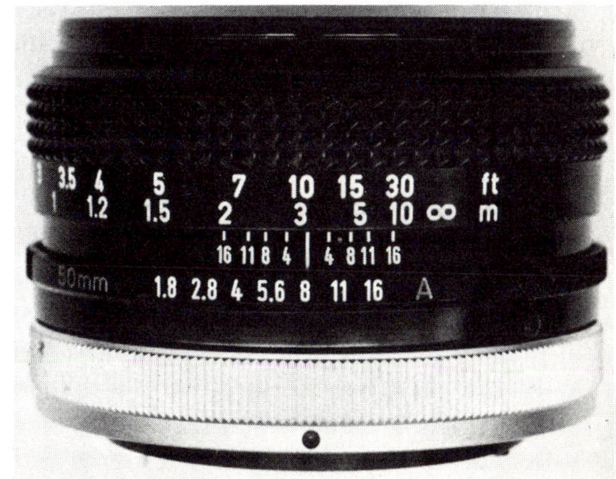

Fig. 5-3. F-stops are marked on a moveable ring on the lens. Each f-stop lets in one-half (or double) the light of the next setting.

	Shutter Speed	Aperture
BRIGHT OR HAZY SUN ON LIGHT SAND OR SNOW. (Distinct shadows, very bright)	1/125 second	f/22
BRIGHT OR HAZY SUN (Distinct shadows)	1/125 second	f/16*
WEAK, HAZY SUN (Soft shadows)	1/125 second	f/11
CLOUDY BRIGHT (No shadows)	1/125 second	f/8
OPEN SHADE OR HEAVY OVERCAST	1/125 second	f/5.6
*Use f/11 if close-up subject is sidelighted or use f/8 for backlighted close-up subjects.		

Fig. 5-4.   Proper exposure for daylight pictures based on Plus X film with an ASA 125.

Figure 5-4 shows the f-stops normally used when pictures are taken outside. Notice that f/22 is used for a very bright day. F/5.6 is used in the shade or on a very cloudy day. Study the chart carefully to see how light relates to f-stops. Check the camera manual to find out how to adjust the f-stop on your camera.

SETTING THE SHUTTER SPEED

The shutter speed determines how long the light is allowed to reach the film. A fast shutter speed such as 500 (1/500th of a second) is used when the subject is moving. A slow shutter speed used in taking a picture of a moving subject causes the subject to be blurred, as shown in view B of Fig. 5-5. In view C, a fast shutter speed "stopped" the action.

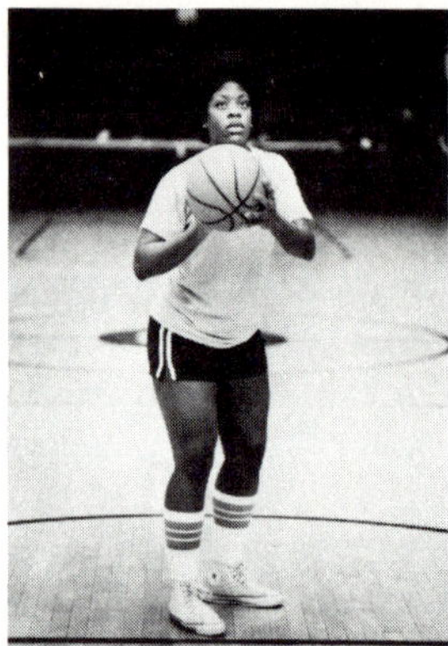

A. A still subject taken at 1/500 of a second with f/2 opening.

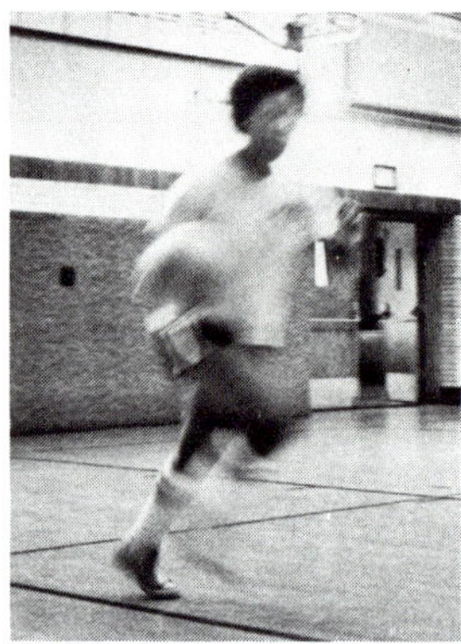

B. Moving subject taken at 1/60 of a second with f/5.6 opening.

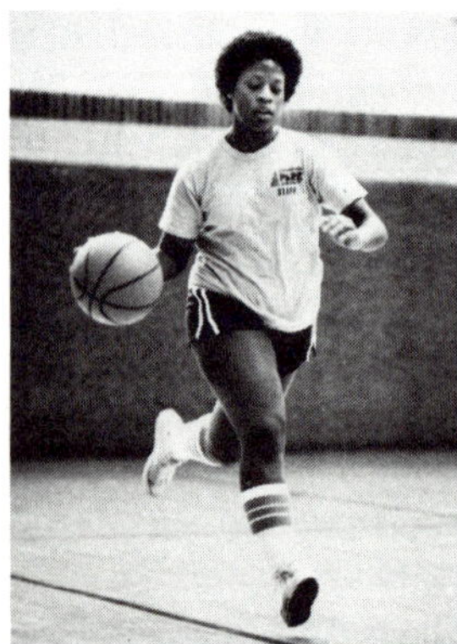

C. Moving subject taken at 1/500 of a second with f/2 opening.

Fig. 5-5.   A fast shutter speed can "stop" the action. Tri X type film was used for these pictures.

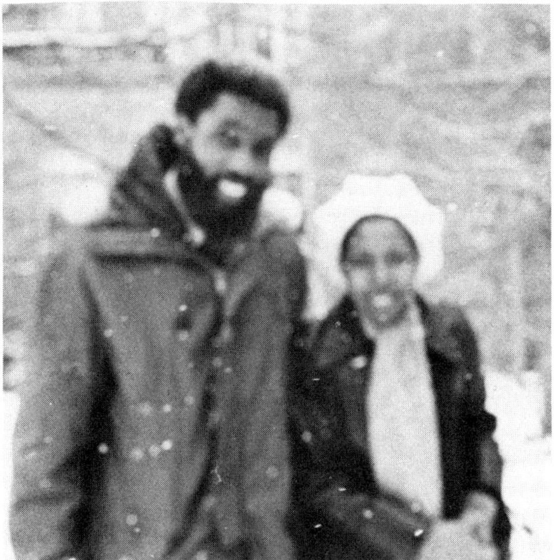

A. Out of focus

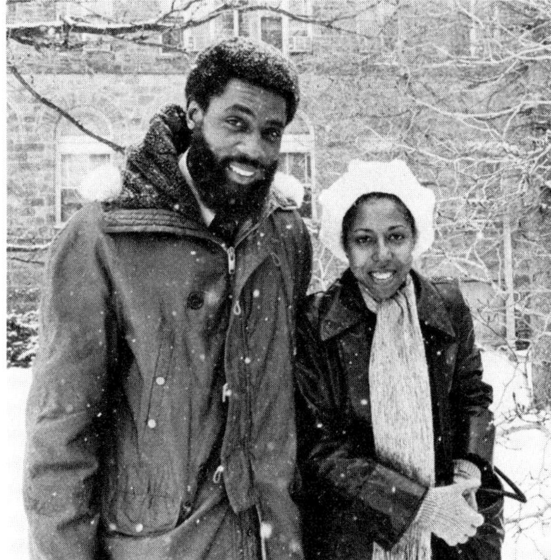

B. In focus

Fig. 5-6.   Be sure your subject is in focus before taking the picture. With a little practice you will learn to focus easily and quickly.

Relating F-Stop with Shutter Speed

The diaphragm and shutter work together to control the light reaching the film. The **faster** the shutter speed, the **larger** the aperture must be. For example, if you are taking a picture of a girl reading, you might set the camera at f/11 at 1/125th of a second. However, if you want a picture of the girl working out on a trampoline, you would need a setting of f/5.6 at 1/500 seconds. In other words, as you increase the shutter speed, you must also increase the light coming into the camera by increasing the f-stop, as shown in Fig. 5-5.

For your first experiences in using a camera, set your shutter speed at 125, 1/125th of a second. This is a good setting for most daytime, outside shooting of still subjects. In later chapters, you will learn more about using fast shutter speeds to take action shots.

FOCUSING

Focusing is a simple, but important part of taking pictures. It is a separate adjustment and not affected by f-stop and shutter speed. When the subject of a picture is out of focus, the result is usually a poor picture, Fig. 5-6.

The focusing device on cameras vary. Look at the camera manual to find out how to adjust the focus. Practice focusing on objects around the room before taking any pictures. This will help you learn to focus quickly.

HOW TO HANDLE A CAMERA

A camera is a fine instrument. Use it carefully. Protect the lens from scratches. The camera "sees through" the lens which means that any scratches will always show up on the picture. Do not touch the lens with your fingers. The oils from your skin smudge the glass. If the lens is dusty, use a camel hair lens brush or some lens cleaner and tissue to clean it.

Learn how to hold the camera properly. It must be held very still while you take the picture. This is doubly important when you use a slow shutter speed. Any movement will cause

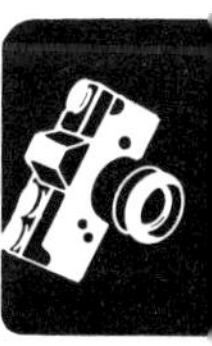

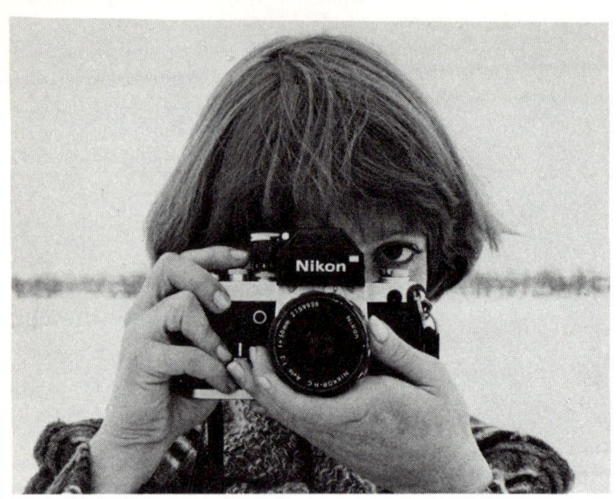

A. Taking a horizontal shot.

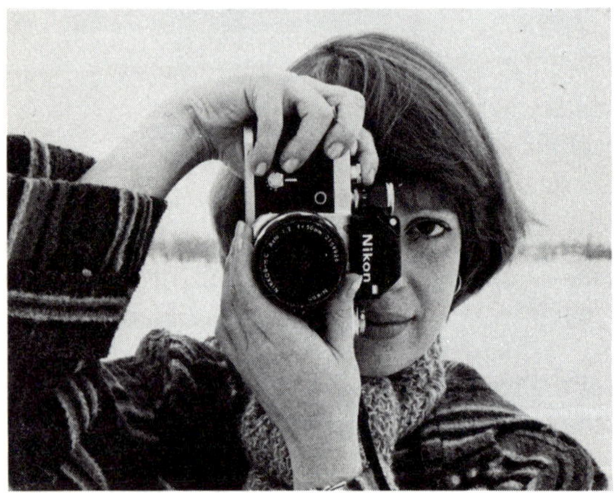

B. Taking a vertical shot.

Fig. 5-7.   Holding the camera properly.

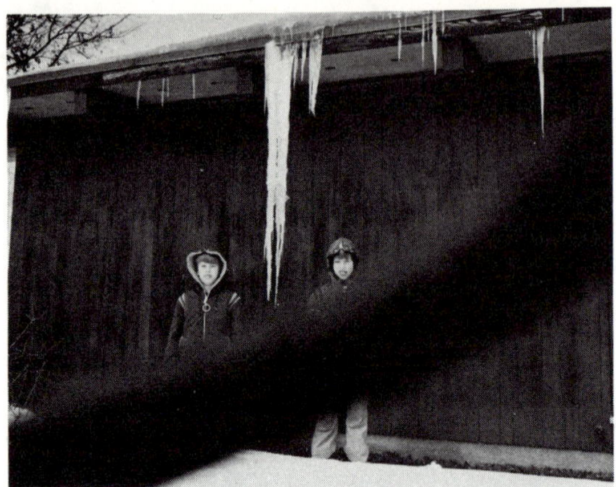

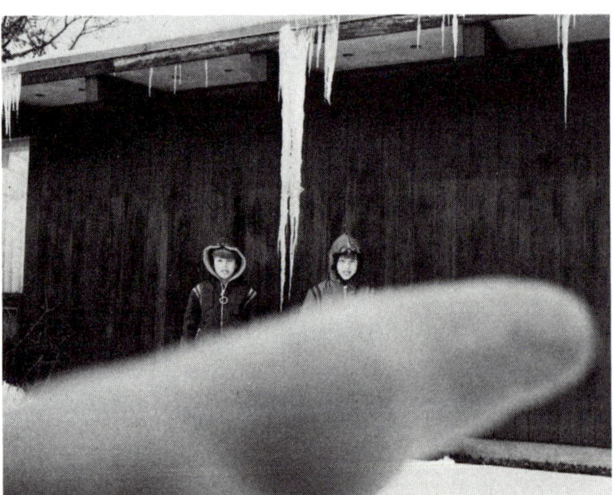

Fig. 5-8.   The results can be disappointing if the camera strap or your fingers get in front of the lens.

the picture to blur. Figure 5-7 shows the proper way to hold a 35 mm camera.

When taking the picture, be sure that your fingers or the camera strap do not get in front of the lens, Fig. 5-8. Also, be sure the lens cap is off before you shoot your picture.

Do not leave the camera in a hot car. The heat could ruin the film and the fine oil in the camera mechanism.

If your camera has a case, store the camera in it. The case protects the camera from dust and bumps.

While using your camera, put the camera strap around your neck or wrist so you do not accidently drop it.

ACTIVITY 5 — TAKING PICTURES

Take 10 pictures outside during the day using Plus X film or any black and white film with an ASA rating of 125. Use a shutter speed of 1/125th of a second. Take some of your pictures in bright sun. Take some of them in the shade. Use the chart in Fig. 5-4 to determine the proper f-stop.

Fig. 5-9.

Photography Record Sheet

Name _________________________ Hour ___________ Assignment No. ___________

Film Type _________________________ ASA _________________________

1. Subject ____

   Shutter speed _________________________ f/ _________________________

2. Subject ____

   Shutter speed _________________________ f/ _________________________

3. Subject ____

   Shutter speed _________________________ f/ _________________________

4. Subject ____

   Shutter speed _________________________ f/ _________________________

5. Subject ____

   Shutter speed _________________________ f/ _________________________

6. Subject ____

   Shutter speed _________________________ f/ _________________________

7. Subject ____

   Shutter speed _________________________ f/ _________________________

8. Subject ____

   Shutter speed _________________________ f/ _________________________

9. Subject ____

   Shutter speed _________________________ f/ _________________________

10. Subject ____

   Shutter speed _________________________ f/ _________________________

Procedure

1. Load the camera with Plus X film (ASA 125).
2. Advance the film twice before taking the first picture if you are not using cartridge film.
3. Supply the following information on the chalkboard and take a picture of it, using a setting of f/2 and shutter speed of 1/30th of a second.

   Your Name

   Class Hour

   Activity 5, Taking Pictures

   Always begin all future camera assignments by taking a picture of your handwritten name, class hour, activity number, and title.
4. Set the shutter speed back to 1/125.
5. Take nine pictures outside during the day. Take some in bright sunlight and some in shade. Use the chart on page 24 to determine the proper f-stop.
6. Keep a record of each shot on a form similar to the one shown in Fig. 5-9. This will help you see any mistakes you are making in taking pictures. Your teacher may make copies of this form for you.
7. If a partner is shooting the other half of the roll of film give him or her the camera.
8. When the roll has been exposed, rewind it and remove the film. Your teacher will show you how to do this. **Do not open the camera or rewind the film** until your teacher gives you instructions. Instamatic cameras do not rewind the film. It is advanced into the other side of the cartridge.

STUDY QUESTIONS

1. Why is it necessary to advance the film twice before taking the first picture?
2. Explain how the size of the aperture changes according to the amount of light available.
3. Explain why a larger f-stop number is a smaller aperture.
4. Explain how the shutter speed and diaphragm work together to control exposure. What must you do to the aperture if you increase shutter speed?
5. List three ways you should protect your camera from damage.

Chapter 6   DEVELOPING ROLL FILM

Roll film is developed in the same way as sheet film except a developing tank is used rather than trays. The tank allows you to work in the light most of the time. Film is put into the tank in complete darkness, but after the tank is closed the light is turned on. The best way to learn to develop a roll of film is to do it. You will now develop the roll of film you used in taking pictures during the last activity.

ACTIVITY 6 — PART I
DEVELOPING ROLL FILM

Assignment

Prepare the following assignment to be handed in to your teacher.
1. 10 negatives from the roll of film you shot in Activity 5.
2. One contact sheet of the negatives.
3. Completed photography record sheet.

Materials Needed

10 frames of Plus X film exposed during Activity 5
Three 5 x 7 in. sheets polycontrast F paper
Darkroom supplies

Loading the Developing Tank

1. Figures 6-1 through 6-4 show how to take the film out of its cassette and put it on a developing reel. This work must be done in **total** darkness. Before attempting this in the darkroom, first practice the procedure shown, using an old strip of film and a developing reel. Make sure you can do the work with your eyes closed before you actually load the tank in the darkroom.
2. When you are well practiced, you are ready to handle your own film. Go into the darkroom. Remove the film from the cassette, thread it on the developing reel and place the reel in the empty developing tank, Fig. 6-5. Replace the lid, making sure it is tight before you turn on the lights.

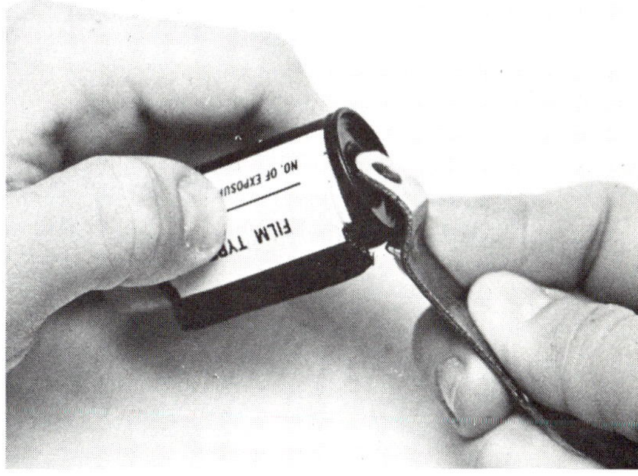

Fig. 6-1.   Be sure the darkroom is completely dark before you remove the film from its cover. Pry off the bottom of a cassette with a bottle opener or cassette opener. Slide the spool out.

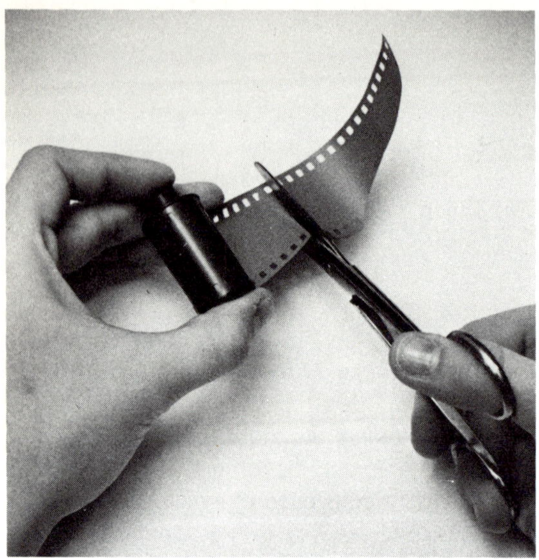

Fig. 6-2.   Handle the film by the edges only. Oils from your skin will cause uneven development. Use the scissors to cut off the end of the film to square it off.

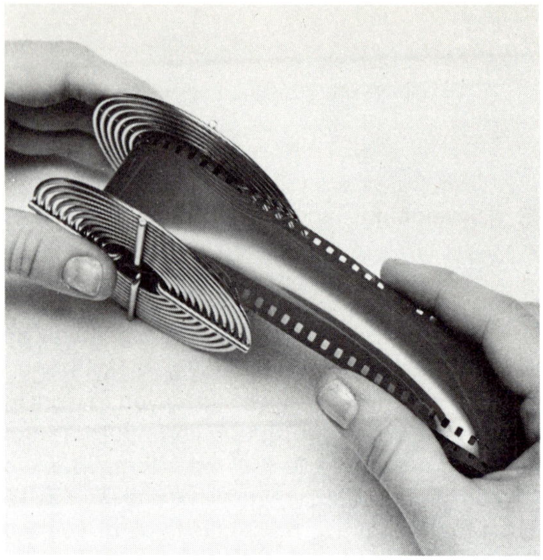

Fig. 6-4.   To finish threading the reel, lay the reel edgewise on the table. Push the film so the reel rolls forward. As it rolls, the reel will pull the film into the grooves. When you reach the end, cut the spool off the end of the film.

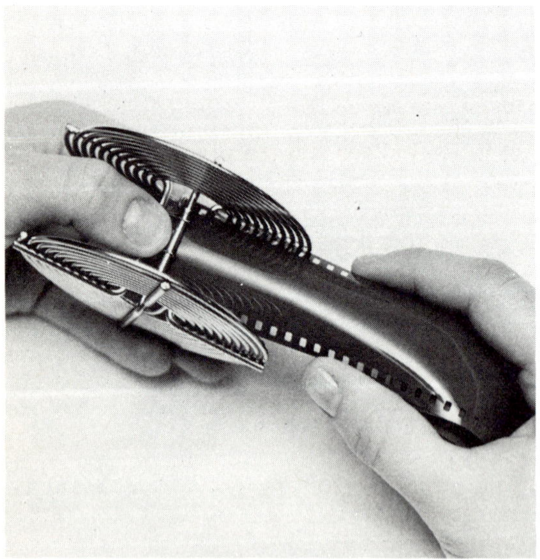

Fig. 6-3.   Hold the spool so that film unwinds off the top. Unwind a short piece and bow it between your thumb and forefinger. Thread the film into the reel.

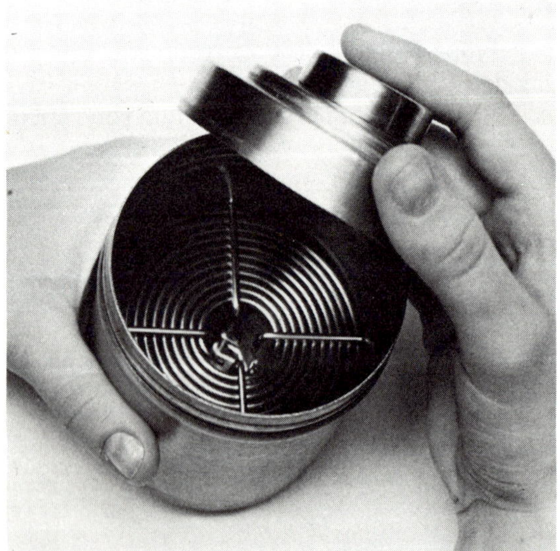

Fig. 6-5.   Place the reel in the developing tank and put on the cover. Be sure the cover is on properly before turning on the lights.

Developing the Film

1. Prepare the developer according to instructions on the package. Check the temperature of the developer. Be prepared to start the timer as soon as you fill the tank.

2. Choose the proper length of time for developing, according to the following chart.

Temperature		Time
°F	°C	
65°	18.3°	6-1/2 min.
68°	20 °	5-1/2 min.
70°	21.1°	4-3/4 min.
72°	22.2°	4-1/2 min.
75°	23.9°	3-1/4 min.

Fill the tank with developer, pouring it through the special opening at the top, Fig. 6-6. Start the timer. Tap the bottom of the tank five times with your hand to clear any air bubbles that may be on the film.

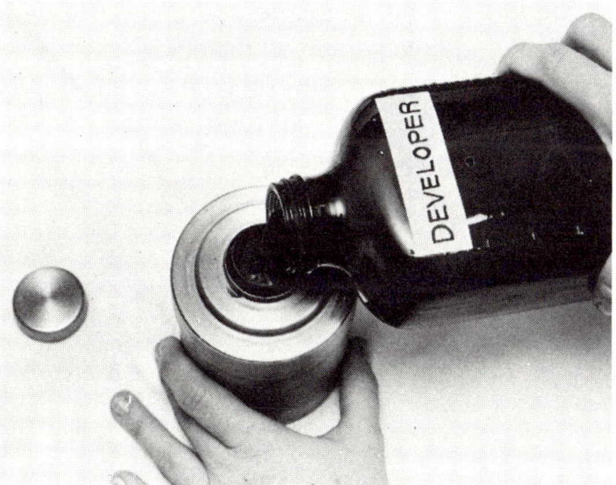

Fig. 6-6.   Pour in the developer and start the timer. Be sure to replace the pouring cap. Tap the bottom of the tank five times to clear the air bubbles. All steps in the developing process are done while the film is in the tank. All chemicals are poured through the same opening at the top. Do not remove the cover until development is complete.

3. While the film is developing, agitate for 5 seconds every 30 seconds. Figure 6-7 shows two ways to agitate a developing tank. If you are not using either of these two types of tanks, your teacher will show you how to agitate your tank.

4. When the time is up, remove the **cap** on the cover and pour out the developer. Your teacher will tell you where to pour it.

5. Pour the stop bath in the tank. Its temperature should be at 65° to 70° F (18° to 21° C). Agitate for 30 seconds. Remove

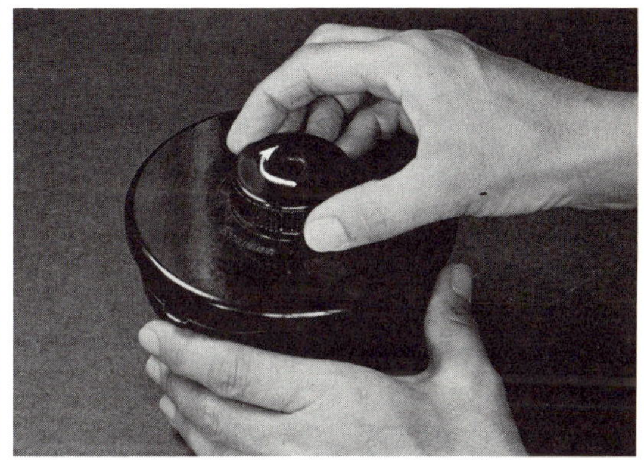

A. Agitating by turning small knob on tank.

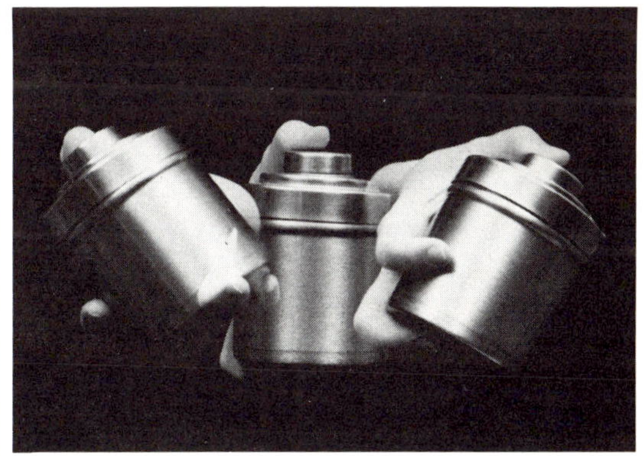

B. Agitating by repeatedly turning the tank upside down and back again.

Fig. 6-7.   Correct methods for agitating a developing tank. Follow your teacher's instructions for the type of tank you use.

the cap and pour out the stop bath according to your teacher's instructions.

6. Pour the fixer in the tank. Its temperature should be between 65° F and 75° F (18° and 24° C). Leave in the tank for 8-10 minutes. Agitate every 30 seconds. After 8-10 minutes, pour out the fixer according to your teacher's instructions.

7. Take the top off the tank and fill the tank with water to remove the fixer. Pour out the water into the sink.

8. Pour hypo clear in the tank. Agitate for 30 seconds. Pour out the hypo clear as instructed by your teacher.

9. Wash your film in running water for 5 minutes. Do **not** turn the water on full force.

10. Remove the film from the developing reel and hang to dry.

11. Your negatives will be ready for printing when dry.

Cleaning Up

1. Clean the tank and reel with running water. Return them to their proper place.

2. Return all chemicals to their proper places.

3. Wipe up any excess water. Generally clean the area.

PART 2 — MAKING A CONTACT PRINT

1. Cut the negatives into two strips of four frames and one of two frames.

2. Remove any dust from the negatives with an antistatic brush. Handle the negatives by the edges to avoid getting fingerprints on them.

3. Clean the printing frame glass and insert the negatives with the emulsion side **down.**

4. Place the printing frame on the enlarger and turn the enlarger on. Adjust the enlarger head until the light covers the negatives. Turn the light off.

5. Turn off the regular lights and turn on the safelight.

6. Place a piece of 5″ x 7″ printing paper in the printing frame. The **shiny** side of the paper must be **facing** the emulsion (dull) side of the negatives. Close the frame.

7. Set the enlarger lens at f/8. Turn on the lamp for 5 seconds.

8. Develop the contact print for 1-1/2 minutes the same way that you developed your photogram.

9. Turn in to your teacher your contact print, negatives, and photo record sheet. Be sure your negatives are in an envelope so they do not get damaged. Several types of envelopes are available for storage and filing of negatives.

Chapter 7   # PROPER EXPOSURE

Did you have any overexposed or underexposed pictures on your first roll of film? See Fig. 7-1. Getting the correct exposure is a skill that is learned through practice.

You have already learned how shutter speed and f-stop are related in getting the proper exposure. Many factors must be considered to select the correct f-stop, Fig. 7-2:

1. Type of day — sunny or cloudy.
2. Background — light or dark.
3. Source of light — front or back.
4. Distance — close or far away.
5. Subject — light colored or dark colored.

These conditions all affect your choice of f-stop. You may need to use either a smaller f-stop, called **stop down,** or a larger f-stop, called **stop up.** For example, with a bright background you would adjust from f/8 to f/11 or stop down the aperture.

One easy reference to use when figuring the speed and f-stop to use is to take 1/ASA rating for speed and f/16 for a sunny day and make your adjustments from that point. Suppose your film has an ASA of 125. You would set the shutter speed at 1/125 of a second (125). An f/16 setting is a good general setting for a

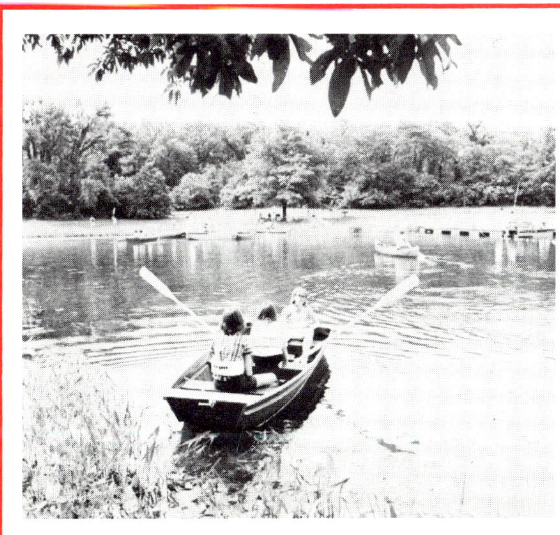

A. Underexposed — f-stop 22, shutter speed 1/1000.

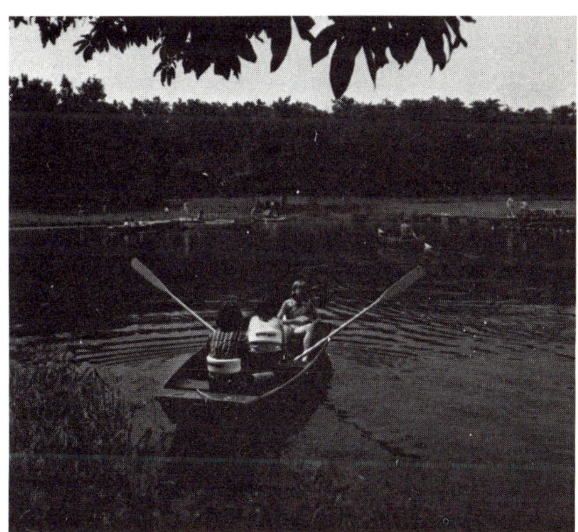

B. Overexposed — f-stop 22, shutter speed 1/125.

Fig. 7-1.   These poor pictures are due to improper exposure. What f-stops and shutter speed would you use for better pictures?

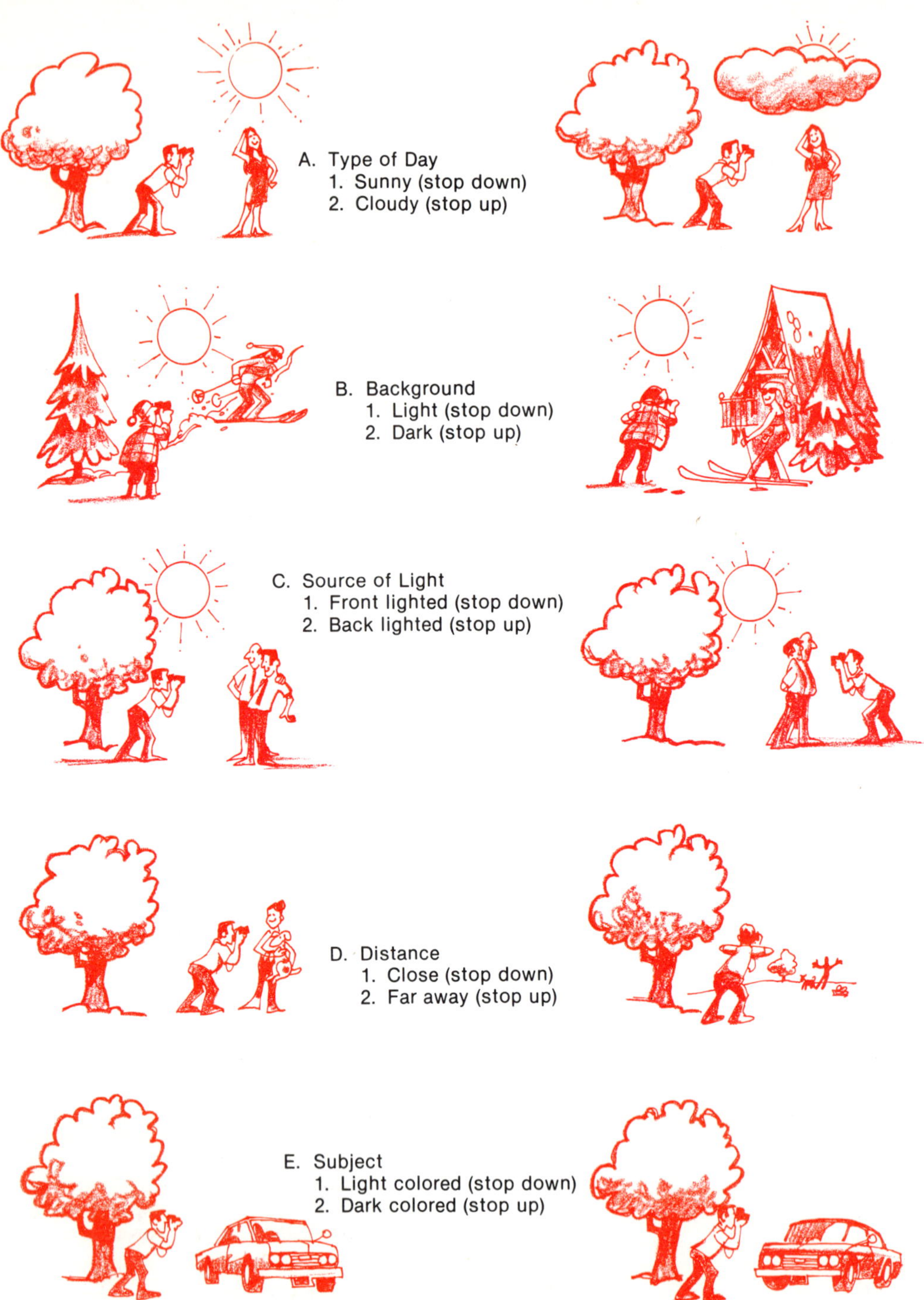

Fig. 7-2.   Factors that determine the proper f-stop setting.

sunny day. If you are shooting pictures on a cloudy day or on a bright day in snow, you would stop up or stop down from f/16. Look at the chart in Fig. 7-3. It shows how to adjust the f-stop to different situations with **front-lighted** subjects. The colored central square is the reference point. When a square shows +2 f-stops, **it means to open up two stops from f/16 to f/8.** The shutter speed stays the same under all conditions except where noted. Study the chart carefully until you understand it. As you gain experience with judging f-stops, keep a copy of the chart with your camera for easy reference.

Front lighted subjects face the light source. In some situations, the light comes from the side or behind the subject. This is called **side lighting** or **back lighting.** Figure 7-4 shows the difference among the three light sources. Compare this to Fig. 7-5. Although the chart in Fig. 7-3 applies to front lighted subjects, you can make adjustments for back and side lighting. As noted at the bottom of the chart, you would open up 2 f-stops for back lighting and 1 f-stop for side lighting on sunny days. The direction of your light source is not of concern on cloudy days. The chart shows you that a close subject on a sunny day with distinct shadows requires f/11 at 125. However, if the subject were backlighted, you must stop up 2 f-stops to a setting of f/5.6. Study the chart carefully until you understand how to adjust for back and side lighting.

Fig. 7-3

Exposure Chart for Front Lighted Subjects

Unless shown otherwise, shutter speed is 1/125.
Readings are for a front-lighted subject.

	Bright or Hazy Sun *	Bright or Hazy Sun *	Light Cloudy	Dull Cloudy	Heavy Overcast or Open Shade
Light or Distant Subject	− 2 f-stops 1/250 at f/22 or 1/500 at f/16	− 1 f-stop f/22 or 1/250 at f/16	$\frac{1}{ASA}$ sec. at f/16	+ 1 f-stop f/11	+ 2 f-stops f/8
Average or Nearby Subject	− 1 f-stop f/22	$\frac{1}{ASA}$ sec. at f/16	+ 1 f-stop f/11	+ 2 f-stops f/8	+ 3 f-stops f/5.6
Dark or Closeup Subject	$\frac{1}{ASA}$ sec. at f/16	+ 1 f-stop f/11	+ 2 f-stops f/8	+ 3 f-stops f/5.6	+ 4 f-stops f/4
	On Sand or Snow	Distinct Shadows	Soft Shadows	No Shadows	No Shadows

* For back lighting, step up 2 f-stops.
* For side lighting, step up 1 f-stop.

Closeups require more exposure because shadow details are more important.

Example of exposure: Average object with light giving distinct shadows.

$\frac{1}{ASA}$ f/16   If ASA is 125, then use $\frac{1}{125}$ sec. at f/16.

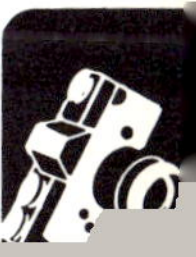

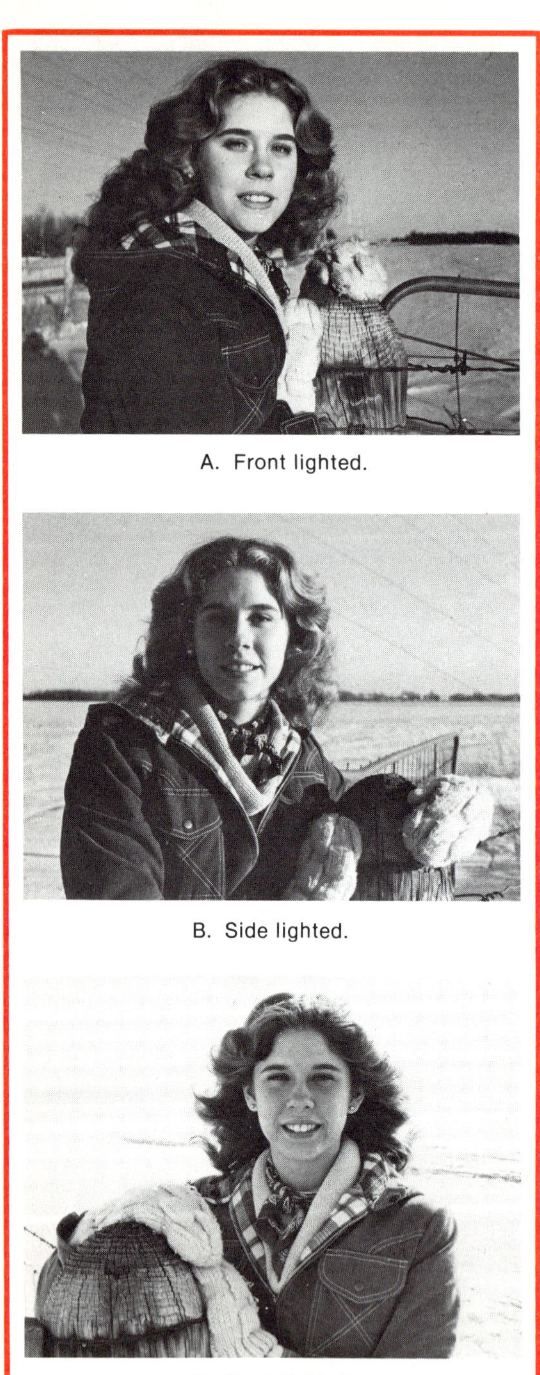

A. Front lighted.

B. Side lighted.

C. Back lighted.

Fig. 7-4.   There are three sources of light. Generally, you open up two f-stops for backlighting and one f-stop for sidelighting.

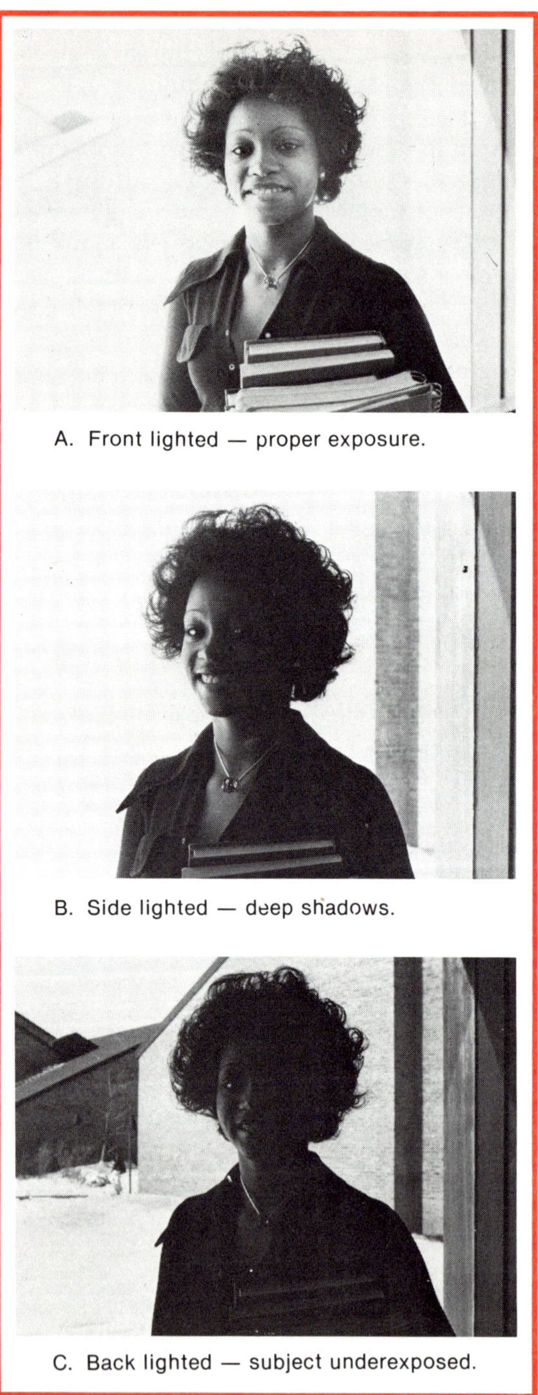

A. Front lighted — proper exposure.

B. Side lighted — deep shadows.

C. Back lighted — subject underexposed.

Fig. 7-5.   The light source was not considered when the pictures were taken having side and back lighting. On very cloudy days, you do not have to worry about light source. Why?

STUDY QUESTIONS

1. List five factors to consider when selecting the proper f-stop.
2. Why is it important to consider the background when selecting f-stop?
3. If you are using ASA 125 film, what shutter speed would you use as a point of reference?
4. What is a good general f-stop for a bright sunny day?
5. If it is cloudy, would you set the aperture at a smaller or larger f-stop? Why?
6. Explain the difference between front, back, and side lighting. Also, explain how and why the source of light affects the f-stop you choose.

ACTIVITY 7 — TAKING PICTURES AND MAKING CONTACT PRINTS

Assignment

Prepare to hand in the following assignment.
1. Ten negatives to be graded on cleanliness and proper development.
2. Contact prints to be graded on proper exposure of pictures and quality of development.
3. Completed photography record sheet.

Materials Needed

Plus X film
1 sheet 5 x 7 in. polycontrast F paper
Darkroom supplies

Taking the Pictures

1. **Frame 1.** Take a picture of your name, class hour, and assignment number written on the chalkboard, using a setting of f/2 at 1/30 of a second.
2. Turn your shutter speed back to 125.
3. Keep a record of each shot on your photo record sheet.
4. Choose either Plan A or Plan B picture assignment.

Plan A — For a Bright Day

Take pictures as follows:
Frame 2 — A light, average, or dark object front-lighted by the sun.
Frame 3 — A light, average, or dark object back-lighted by the sun.
Frame 4 — A light, average, or dark object in open shade.
Frame 5 — A light, average, or dark object in covered shade (under the shade of a tree or overhang of a building).

Frames 6-10 will be used to show the difference in exposure that one and two f-stops will make. Shoot the same object for each picture at the same distance from the camera. Determine the correct exposure for your subject and follow the directions below. Taking these pictures in shade will allow you to use the full range of f-stops.

Frame 6 — Stop down two f-stops from correct exposure.
Frame 7 — Stop down one f-stop from correct exposure.
Frame 8 — Correct exposure.
Frame 9 — Stop up one f-stop from correct exposure.
Frame 10 — Stop up two f-stops from correct exposure.

Plan B — For a Cloudy Day

Take pictures as follows:
Frame 2 — A light object in full skylight.
Frame 3 — A dark object in full skylight.
Frame 4 — A light object in covered shade.
Frame 5 — A dark object in covered shade.

Follow the instructions for frame 6-10 under plan A.

Developing and Printing

1. Develop the film, using the same procedure you used in developing your previous roll of Plus X film. See pages 31-32.
2. Make a contact print of your negatives. See page 32 for procedures.
3. Turn in your negatives, contact prints, and record sheet to your teacher.

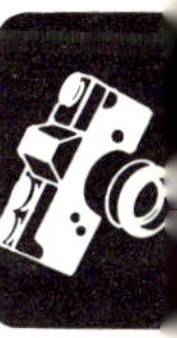

MAKING AN ENLARGEMENT

Chapter 8

An enlargement is a print that is larger than the negative, Fig. 8-1. Common enlargement sizes are 3-1/2″ x 5″, 5″ x 7″, 8″ x 10″, and 11″ x 14″. An enlargement is made by using the same procedure as in making contact prints, with two exceptions. First, only one negative is used at a time to make an enlargement. Second, the negative does not come in contact with the photographic paper. When a negative is placed in the enlarger's negative carrier, light projecting through the negative onto photographic paper enlarges the picture. Study Fig. 8-2. The farther away the negative is from the paper, the larger the enlargement will be.

An enlargement is made according to these steps:

1. Prepare the chemicals for making a print.
2. Select and clean the negative you wish to enlarge.
3. Place the negative in the enlarger's negative carrier.
4. Select a polycontrast filter (if using polycontrast paper).
5. Place the negative carrier in the enlarger.
6. Focus the image on the easel. The lens should be wide open.
7. Adjust the aperture.
8. Prepare to make a test strip.

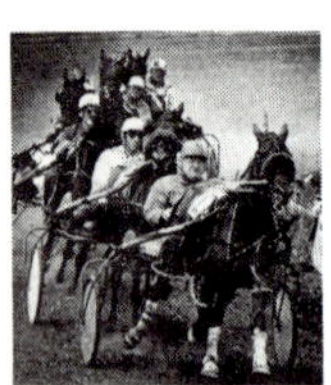 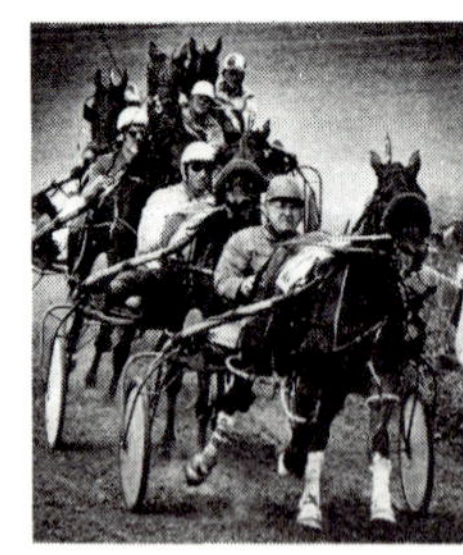 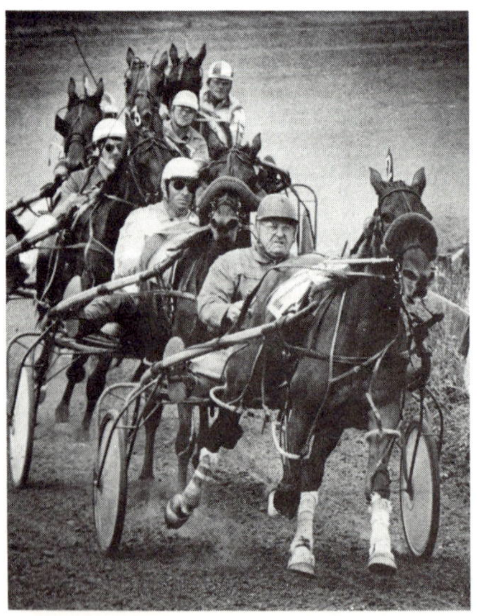

Fig. 8-1.   Many different sizes of enlargements can be made from a negative.

9. Make a test strip.
10. Develop the test strip.
11. Look at the test print and determine the best exposure time.

12. Make the final print.

Figures 8-3 through 8-17 show how an enlargement is made.

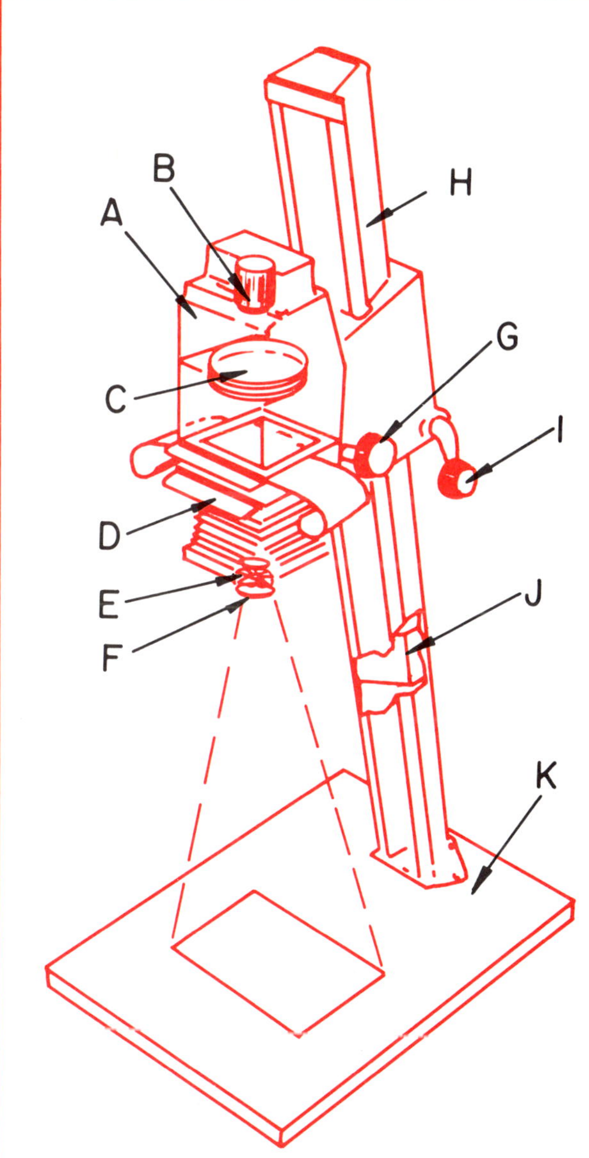

A. The enlarger head holds the main working parts: the light source, negative carrier, and lenses. The head moves up and down to determine the size of the enlargement. The higher the head, the larger the picture will be.

B. The lamp, similar to the common lightbulb, supplies the light to expose the photographic paper. The light shines through the negative and onto the paper.

C. The condensor lens is a pair of convex elements. The lens spreads the light over the negative. Enlargers having no condensor lens use another method of diffusing the light.

D. The negative carrier is located between the condensor and main lens and holds the negative flat and level.

E. The diaphragm is an adjustable opening like that on a camera. It controls the amount of light passing through the lens to the paper.

F. The lens bends the light rays passing through the negative to make an enlarged picture.

G. The focusing control moves the lens up or down to focus the picture on the paper.

H. The supporting column holds the enlarged head out over the baseboard and printing paper. The head can be moved up and down on the column.

I. The height adjustment raises or lowers the enlarger head to determine the picture size.

J. The counterbalance, usually inside the column, balances the weight of the enlarger head so it can be moved up and down easily.

K. The baseboard is the foundation that holds the enlarger. The easel on which the photographic paper is placed is on the baseboard.

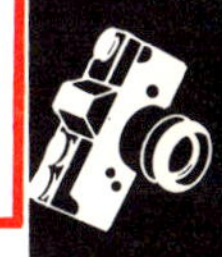

Fig. 8-2.   How the parts of an enlarger work.

STEP 1 — PREPARING THE CHEMICALS

The same chemicals are used to make an enlargement as to make the photogram or contact sheet. In review, the steps in making an enlargement are:

1. Developer
2. Stop Bath (Acetic Acid & water)
3. Fixer (hypo)
4. Hypo clear*
5. Wash
6. Treat with Pakosol to prevent spotting*
7. Dry

***Note:** If you use resin coated (RC) paper, you will not need to do steps 4 and 6. Also, RC paper should be air dried. Do not place this type of paper in a hot drier. The image will be damaged.

STEP 2 — SELECTING AND CLEANING THE NEGATIVE

The negative should be free of dust, dirt, and fingerprints, Fig. 8-5. Remove any dust from the negative with a camel-hair brush or canned air, Fig. 8-6. Remove dirt or fingerprints with film cleaner and a soft cloth rag (not paper). The negative can also be treated with Photo-Flo® while you gently rub it with your fingers. Any dust not removed from the negative will show up as specks or blotches on the print. Be careful not to scratch the negative as you clean it.

STEP 3 — PLACING THE NEGATIVE IN THE CARRIER

Place the clean negative in the negative carrier, emulsion side (dull side) down, Fig. 8-7. Turn the negative upside down in the carrier so that the image will appear right side up on the enlarging easel. **Do not pull** the negative through the carrier. This will scratch it. Open the carrier when moving the film to another frame or when centering the frame.

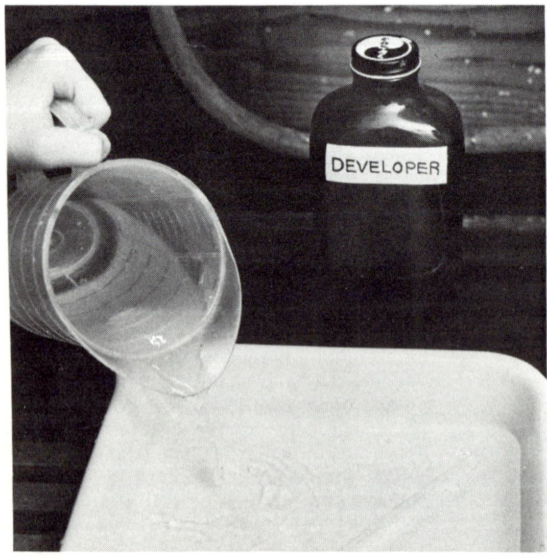

Fig. 8-3.   Prepare the chemicals for making a print.

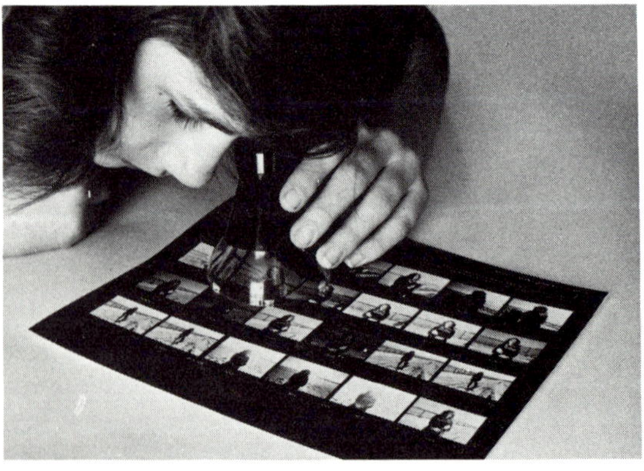

Fig. 8-4.   Choose the negative you wish to enlarge. A magnifying glass can help you choose the best one from your contact prints.

STEP 4 – SELECTING A POLY-CONTRAST FILTER

If you use polycontrast paper in class, you may need to use polycontrast filters. A normal contrast negative requires a #2 polycontrast filter for proper exposure. The filter should be free of dust and smudges. These filters are purchased in a set of #1, #1-1/2, #2, #2-1/2, #3, #3-1/2, and #4 values. When used according to accompanying instructions, they vary the sensitivity of the print paper. The #4 filter increases contrast of underexposed negatives. The #1 filter aids in the printing of overexposed negatives.

STEP 5 – PLACING THE CARRIER IN THE ENLARGER

Place the negative carrier in the enlarger. Open the lens to its largest opening. All lights but safelights should be off.

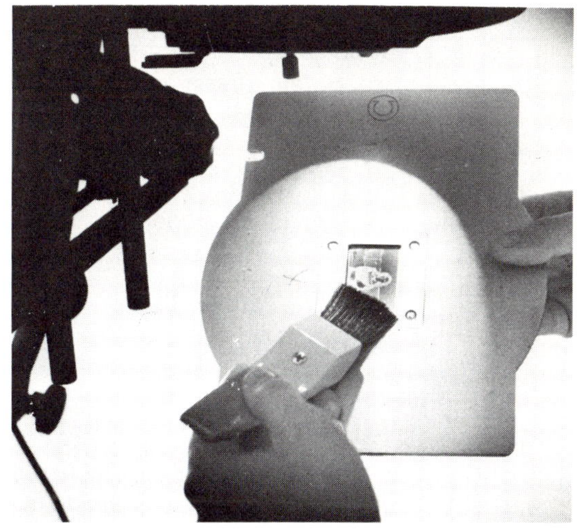

Fig. 8-6.   Hold the negative in the light and check for dust. Brush it off with a camel-hair brush.

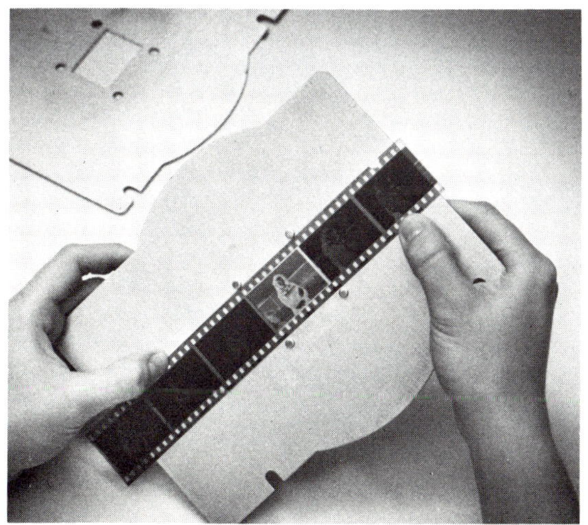

Fig. 8-5.   Put the negative in the negative carrier. If it is dirty or smudged, clean it first.

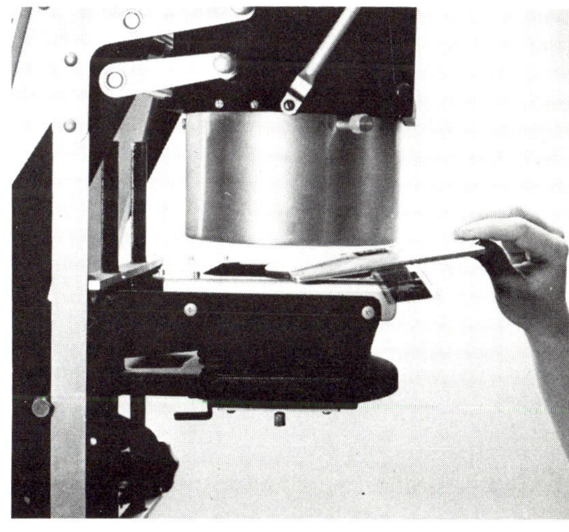

Fig. 8 7.   Place the negative carrier in the enlarger.

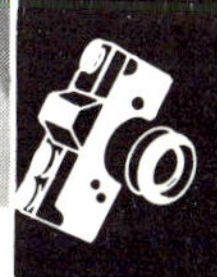

STEP 6 — FOCUSING THE IMAGE ON THE EASEL

Raise or lower the enlarger head until the picture is the size desired, in this case 5″ x 7″, Fig. 8-8. Move the easel around to crop out parts of the picture to obtain better composition. Pick out any sharp area such as an eye, line, or lettering and bring it into focus by adjusting the focusing knob, Fig. 8-9. The image is brighter for focusing if the lens is wide open.

STEP 7 — ADJUSTING THE APERTURE

Stop down the aperture to f/8 or f/11, Fig. 8-10. Do this by stopping down all the way and then opening up one or two stops. How much you open the diaphragm depends on how dense or dark your negative is. Stop down until fine detail begins to fade. A setting of f/11 or f/8 is a good place to start when you determine proper exposure for a normal negative.

STEP 8 — PREPARING TO MAKE A TEST STRIP

You will save time and paper by making a test strip or print. With the safelight on, place a small sheet of photographic paper (about 2″ x 5″) in the enlarger's easel, Fig. 8-11. Be sure the emulsion (shiny) side is up. Have ready a piece of cardboard or other opaque paper the same size or larger than your photographic paper.

STEP 9 — MAKING A TEST STRIP

The test strip you will make is similar to the one done in Chapter 4. See Figs. 8-12A and 8-12B. Follow these directions carefully.

a. Expose the full sheet of paper 3 seconds.
b. Working from the **left-hand** side, cover 1/5 of the paper and expose 3 more seconds.
c. Cover 2/5 of the paper and expose 6 more seconds.

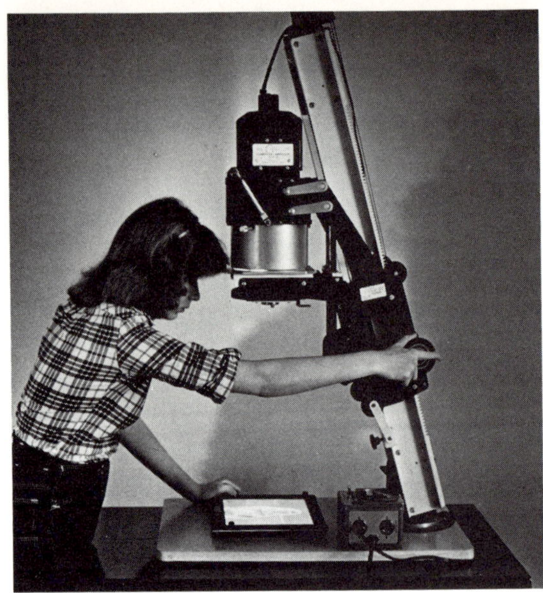

Fig. 8-8.   Working only under the safelight, adjust the enlarger head to get the proper size picture.

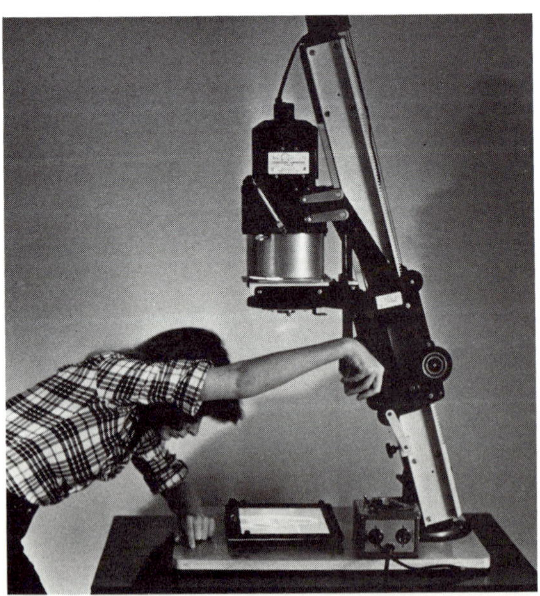

Fig. 8-9.   Focus so that the picture on the easel is sharp and clear. Room light should be off so you can see the picture through the enlarger.

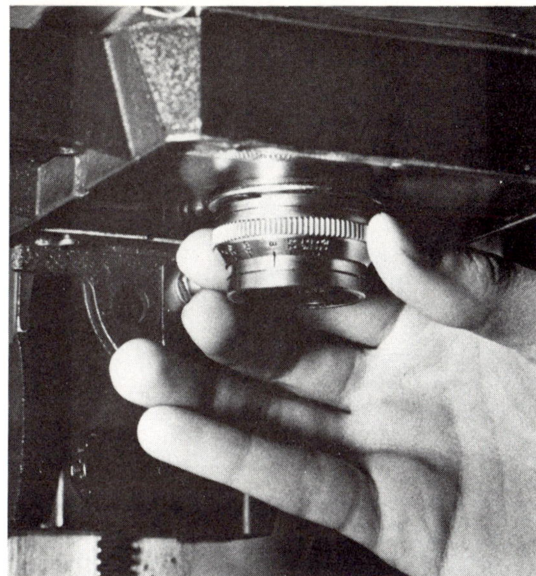

Fig. 8-10. After focus is sharp, adjust the aperture to f/8 or f/11.

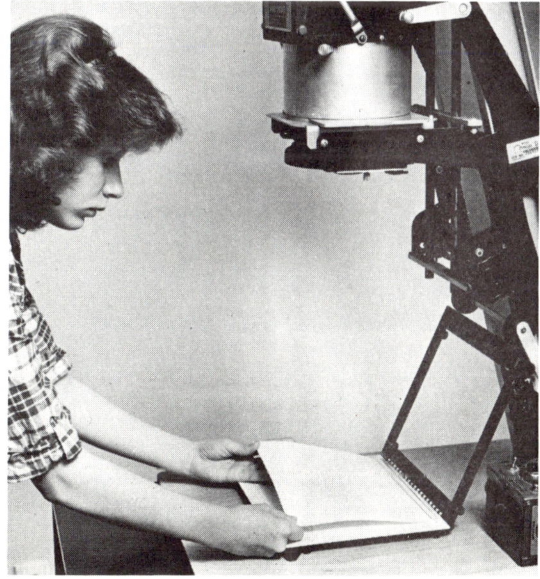

Fig. 8-11. With only the safelight on, slip a strip of photographic paper in the easel, emulsion side up.

d. Cover 3/5 of the paper and expose 12 more seconds.

e. Cover 4/5 of the paper and expose 24 more seconds.

Each section receives twice the light as the previous section.

STEP 10 — DEVELOPING THE TEST STRIP

Develop the print for 1-1/2 minutes. Put the print in the stop bath and then in the fixer for about 1 minute each. See Fig. 8-13.

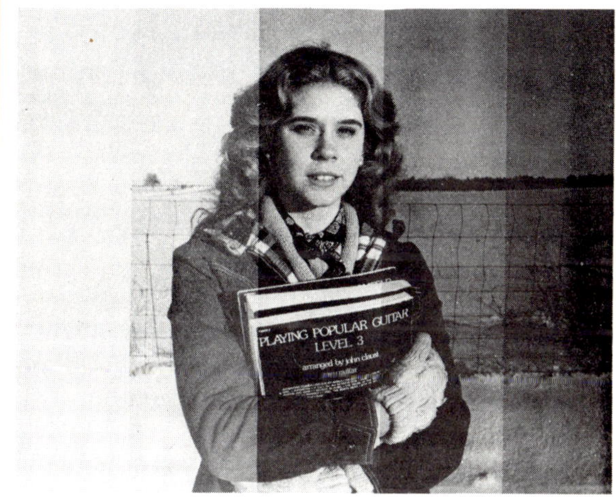

A. Exposing the paper.

Seconds of Exposure

1st	3	3	3	3	3
2nd		3	3	3	3
3rd			6	6	6
4th				12	12
5th					24
Total Sec.	3	6	12	24	48

B. Determining exposure time. Notice that each exposure doubles the previous exposure time.

Fig. 8-12. Make a test strip to determine proper exposure.

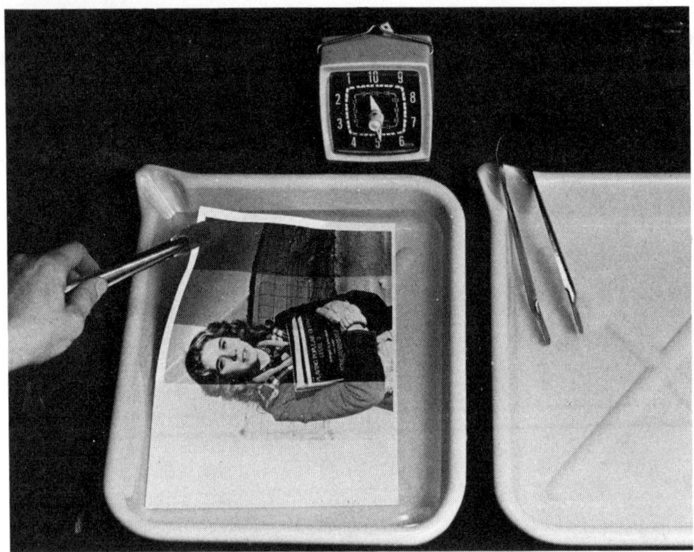

Fig. 8-13.   Develop the test strip and choose the best exposure time.

STEP 11 — EXAMINING THE TEST STRIP

Examine the test strip under the safelight and choose the best exposure. The proper exposure time may lie between two test strip exposures. If the darkest area is too light, a longer time must be used for a test strip or the lens may be opened up one stop. Through experience you will gain ability to make good test strips.

STEP 12 — MAKING THE PRINT

Follow these steps to make your print.

1. Reset the timer as determined by the test print.
2. Recheck the focus and inspect the negative for dust.
3. Place a new piece of paper in the easel.
4. Expose the paper, Fig. 8-14.
5. Process the print, Fig. 8-15. Dry the print according to your teacher's instructions, Figs. 8-16 and 8-17.

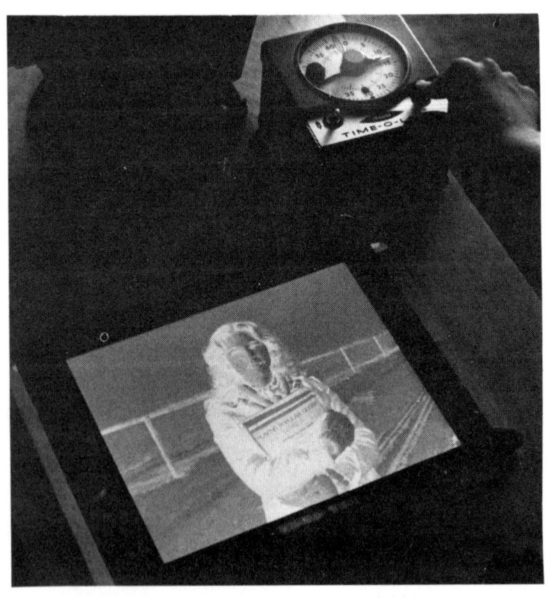

Fig. 8-14. To make the actual print, use the exposure time as determined by the test strip.

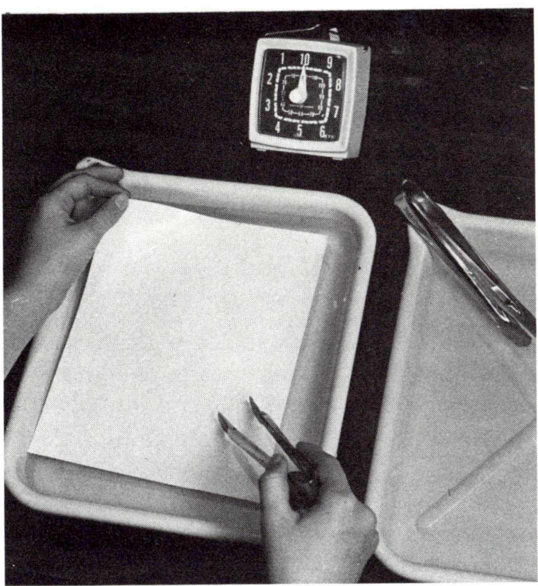

Fig. 8-15. Develop the print immediately.

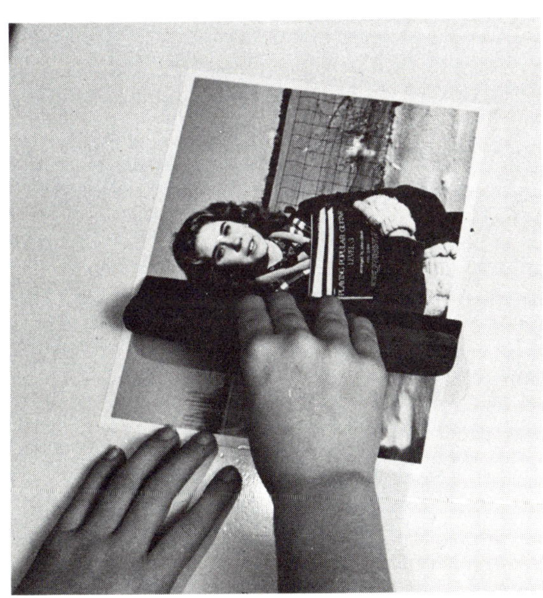

Fig. 8-16. After the final rinse, place the print on a clean, flat surface and remove most of the water from the front and back.

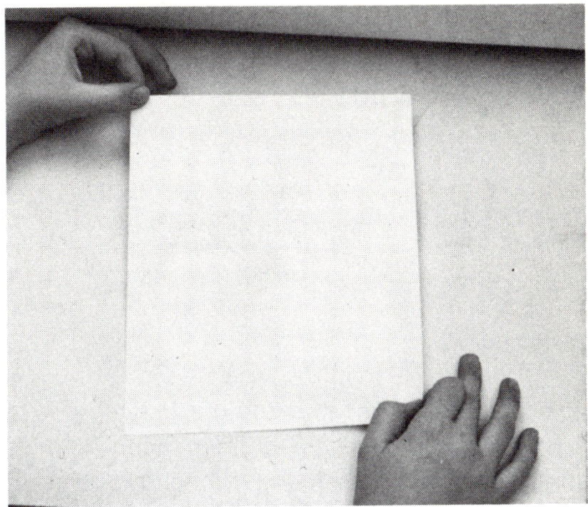

Fig. 8-17. Dry your print by using a blotter or the method commonly used in your classroom.

STUDY QUESTIONS

1. What is an enlargement?
2. Briefly explain how an enlargement is made.
3. Explain why it is important to clean the negative before making an enlargement.
4. Briefly explain why a test strip is necessary. How is one made?

ACTIVITY 8 — MAKING AN ENLARGEMENT

Assignment

Prepare to hand in the following assignment.

1. A 5″ x 7″ enlargement from the negative of your choice.
2. The negative.
3. The test strip used to determine exposure time.

Supplies

Two 5 x 7 in. sheets polycontrast F paper.
Dark room equipment

Follow the steps you have learned to make your enlargement.

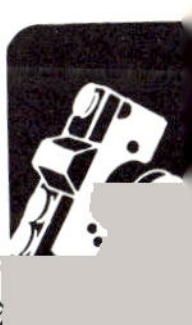

DEPTH OF FIELD

Chapter 9

Depth of field is the area that is in focus in front of and behind the subject that is also in focus. Compare views A and B in Fig. 9-1. Pin #7 in both pictures is in focus. Note, however, how much the depth of field changes when the aperture is changed from f/2 to f/16.

Depth of field is determined by two factors:
1. Aperture (f-stop), and
2. Distance from the subject.

The smaller the aperture, the longer the depth of field. For example, a setting of f/16 has a longer depth of field than f/11. Notice in Fig. 9-1 that view **A** was taken at f/2.8 while view **B** was at f/16.

Distance is also a factor in depth of field. Faraway scenes have a greater depth of field than closeups. Look at the chart in Fig. 9-2. It shows how depth of field relates to distance and f-stop. Notice that if you focus on a subject 10′ away and use a aperture of f/2, everything in the picture from 9′5″ to 10′8″ would be in focus. The depth of field is 1′3″. Now look at the change in depth of focus at a setting of f/16 at 10′. Everything from 6′8″ to 20′3″ would be in focus. This depth of field is 13′7″. (Note that depth of focus is also shown in SI metric numbers.) Study the chart carefully until you see how f-stop and distance affect the depth of field.

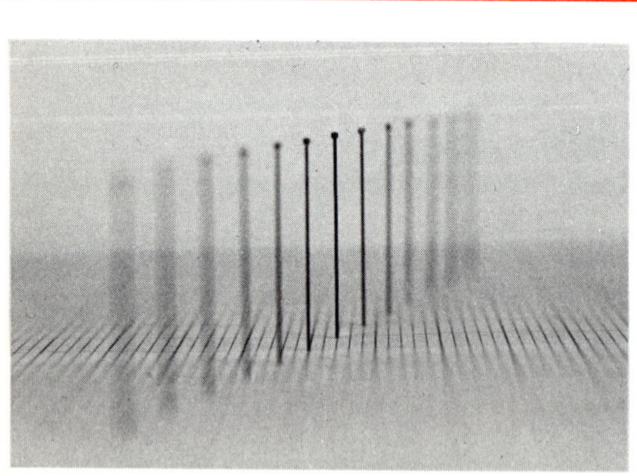

A. Short depth of field. Camera is focused on pin #7 with lens opening at f/2.8 from a distance of 170 mm. Plus X film with ASA of 125 was used.

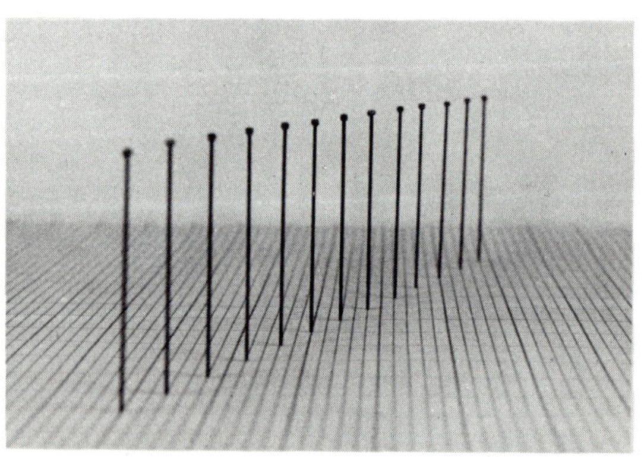

B. Long depth of field. Camera is still focused on pin #7, but f-stop was changed to f/16. Pins in front of and behind pin #7 now also in focus.

Fig. 9-1.   Depth of field refers to the area in focus.

U.S. Customary

	Distance from Focused Subject				
	2′	**5′**	**10′**	**30′**	**∞ (infinity)**
f/2	from 1′ 11.8″ to 2′ 0.2″	from 4′ 10.3″ to 5′ 1.8″	from 9′ 5″ to 10′ 8″	from 25′ to 37′	from 151′ to ∞
	.4″	3.5″	1′ 3″	12′	
f/5.6	from 1′ 11.4″ to 2′ 0.7″	from 4′ 7.4″ to 5′ 5.4″	from 8′ 6″ to 12′ 2″	from 19′ to 66′	from 54′ to ∞
	1.3″	10″	3′ 8″	47′	
f/16	from 1′ 10.3″ to 2′ 2.0″	from 4′ 0.6″ to 6′ 6.8″	from 6′ 8″ to 20′ 3″	from 8′ to 66′	from 19′ to ∞
	3.7″	2′ 6.2″	13′ 7″	58′	

SI Equivalent

	Distance from Focused Subject				
	61 mm	**1.524 m**	**3.048 m**	**9.144 m**	**∞ (infinity)**
f/2	from 604 mm to 614 mm	from 1.475 m to 1.570 m	from 2.870 m to 3.251 m	from 7.62 m to 11.28 m	from 46.03 m to ∞
	10 mm	.095 m	.381 m	3.66 m	
f 5/6	from 594 mm to 628 mm	from 1.407 m to 1.661 m	from 2.591 m to 3.708 m	from 5.79 m to 20.12 m	from 16.46 m to ∞
	34 mm	0.254 m	1.118 m	14.33 m	
f/16	from 0.567 mm to 0.660 mm	from 1.234 m to 2.001 m	from 2.032 m to 6.172 m	from 2.438 m to 20.120 m	from 5.791 m to ∞
	.093 mm	0.767 m	4.14 m	17.682 m	

Example 1: Showing depth of focus for a subject at 10 ft. (3.048) at **f/2.**

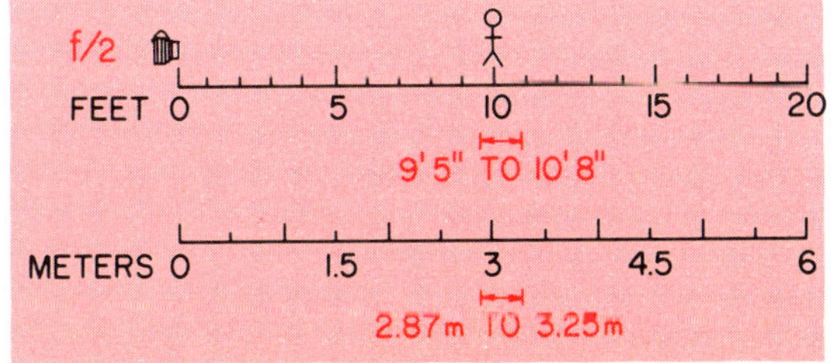

Example 2: Showing depth of focus for a subject at 10 ft. (3.048m) at **f/16.**

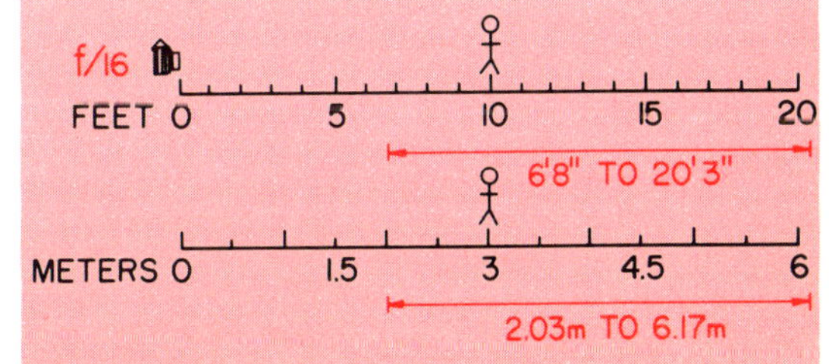

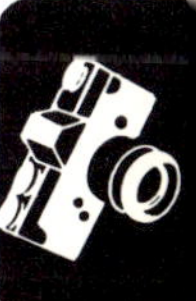

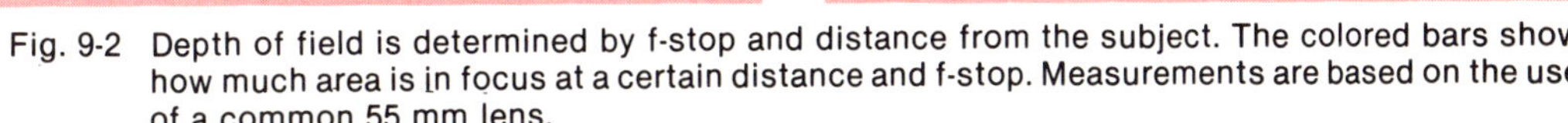

Fig. 9-2 Depth of field is determined by f-stop and distance from the subject. The colored bars show how much area is in focus at a certain distance and f-stop. Measurements are based on the use of a common 55 mm lens.

CONTROLLING THE DEPTH OF FIELD

Since distance from the subject is usually determined by the picture you want, the main control for depth of field is the f-stop. You have already learned that the **f-stop** is determined by the light available. However, you can also control the amount of light reaching the film by the **shutter speed** you choose. The slower the shutter speed, the more light you let into the camera. You can cut down this amount of light by using a smaller aperture. The smaller the aperture, the longer the depth of field. On the other hand, the faster the shutter speed, the more light you need. The aperture must now be made larger which, as a result, shortens the depth of field.

The example below shows how shutter speed and f-stop can be adjusted to change the depth of field.

f/11 at 1/125 sec.
{
f/16 at 1/60 sec.
more depth of field
f/8 at 1/250 sec.
less depth of field
}

Notice that for each stop you increase or decrease the shutter speed, you can make a one-stop increase or decrease in the f-stop.

Camera Symbol	Actual Time	f-stop
1	1 sec.	
2	1/2 sec.	
4	1/4 sec.	
8	1/8 sec.	f/2
16	1/16 sec.	f/2.8
30	1/30 sec.	f/4
60	1/60 sec.	f/5.6
125	1/125 sec.	f/8
250	1/250 sec.	f/11
500	1/500 sec.	f/16
1,000	1/1,000 sec.	f/22

Each shutter speed setting keeps the shutter open one-half the time as the previous speed.

Each f-stop lets in one-half the amount of light as the previous f-stop.

Example Problems

f/16 at 1/60 sec. can be adjusted to f/11 at 1/125 sec.

f/11 at 1/30 sec. can be adjusted to f/5.6 at 1/125 sec.

Complete the following problems, writing your answers on scratch paper:
1. f/5.6 at 1/250 sec. can be adjusted to f/4 at _______ sec.
2. f/11 at 1/125 sec. can be adjusted to f/22 at _______ sec.
3. f/2 at 1/500 sec. can be adjusted to f/8 at _______ sec.
4. f/4 at 1/125 sec. can be adjusted to f/2 at _______ sec.

Fig. 9-3.   Answers to problems: (1) 1/500 (2) 1/60 (3) 1/30 (4) 1/30

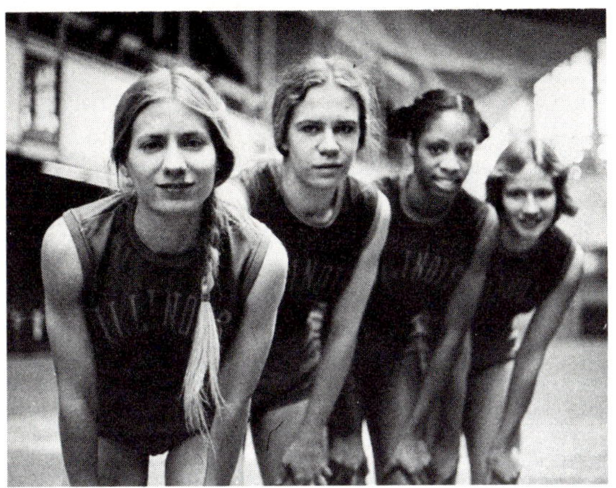

A. A short depth of field calls attention to the subject.

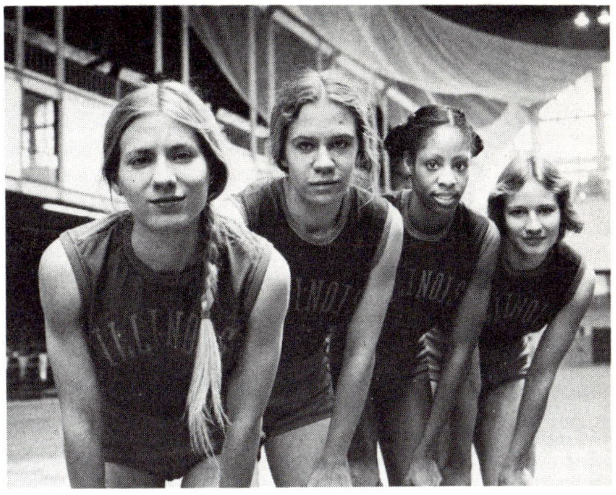

B. A long depth of field brings many details into focus.

Fig. 9-4.   Changing the depth of field.

F/11 at 1/125 can be changed f/16 at 1/60 sec. This increases the depth of field. If you want to decrease the depth of field, you can use f/8 at 1/250 second. The charts in Fig. 9-3 show the f-stop and shutter speed stops commonly found on cameras. Note the example problems showing how f-stop and shutter speed can be adjusted. Make sure you understand how these adjustments are made before starting the problems below the examples. After you have worked the problems, check your answers with those in the Fig. 9-3 caption.

You cannot always control depth of field. If there is very little light, you must shoot at a large aperture and a slow shutter speed to get a picture. You can only get a long depth of field when there is enough light to use a small aperture.

BEING CREATIVE

Being able to choose your depth of field proves useful. You can draw attention to the subject, blurring out everything else, view **A**, Fig. 9-4. Or you can use a longer depth of field to make most of the picture clearly focused, as in view **B**. Depth of field allows you to be creative in taking pictures.

USING DEPTH OF FIELD EFFECTIVELY

Depth of field is greater behind the focused subject than in front of it, Fig. 9-5. For example, when the camera is set at f/5.6 and focused on an object 30′ away, the depth of field is 11′ in front of the subject, but 36′ behind the subject. Refer back to Fig. 9-2. This means that the focused subject is located about 1/3 of the way into the depth of field. Therefore, to get the most effect from depth of field, focus one third of the way into your scene, Fig. 9-6.

Many cameras have a depth of field preview so you can see what is in focus before you take the picture. Check the manual to see whether the camera has a depth of field indicator.

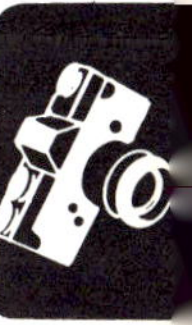

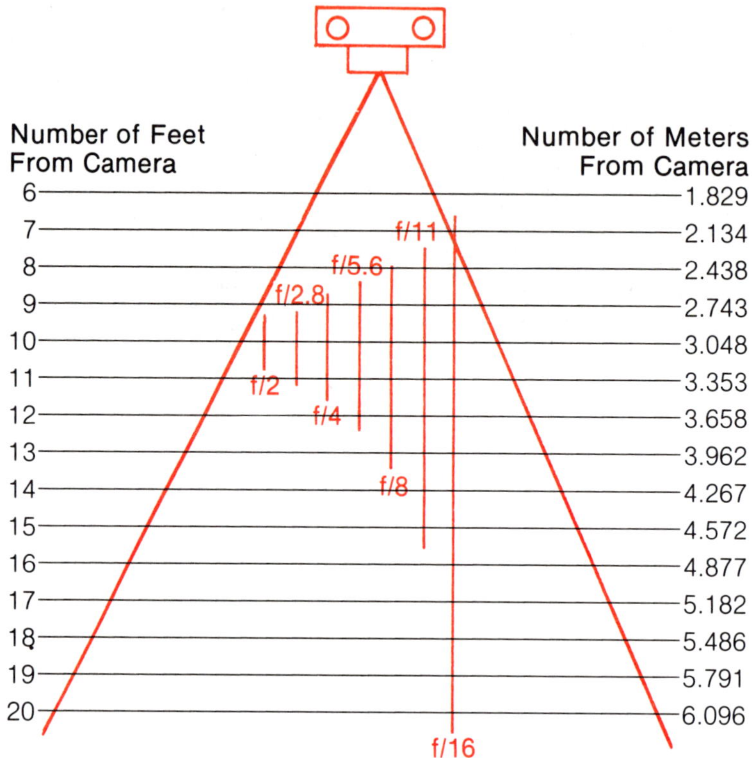

Fig. 9-5.   The vertical lines show the depth of field of the area in focus at different f-stops. Notice that the depth of field is longer behind the focused area than in front of it.

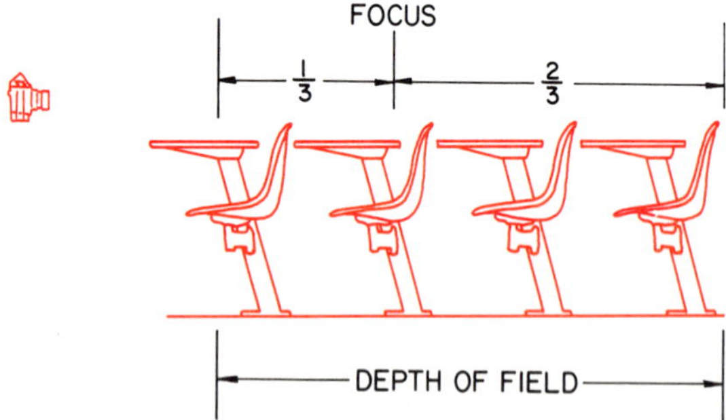

Fig. 9-6.   Generally, the depth of field is one-third in front of the subject and two-thirds behind it. Focusing one-third of the way into the scene will give the greatest depth of field for the f-stop setting.

STUDY QUESTIONS

1. Define depth of field.
2. What two factors determine depth of field? Explain how each relates to depth of field.
3. Explain how shutter speed is related to depth of field.
4. If you stop down the aperture one f-stop, how must you change the shutter speed to get proper exposure?
5. Is the depth of field longer in front of or behind the focused subject?
6. In what instance would you not be able to control depth of field?

ACTIVITY 9 — DEPTH OF FIELD

Assignment

Prepare to hand in the following assignment.

1. Negatives of 10 exposures from roll of Plus X film.
2. Contact sheet of exposures.
3. Three 3-1/2 x 5 in. enlargements of either frames 2, 3 and 4 **or** frames 5, 6, and 7.
4. Exposure record sheet.

Materials Needed

Plus X film
4 sheets 5 x 7 in. polycontrast F paper
Darkroom supplies

Procedure

1. Take 10 pictures according to the following instructions.

Frame 1: Take a picture of your name, hour, assignment number, using f/2 at 1/30 second.

Frames 2, 3 and 4: Use a setting of f/5.6 and the proper speed for correct exposure. (You determine speed by using the chart on page 48 and making adjustments from there.) If you need to review, rework the problems in Fig. 9-3.

	Focus on Subject	Background of wall, fence, or person
Frame 2	2′	6′
Frame 3	5′	6′
Frame 4	15′	6′

Frames 5, 6, and 7: Use the f-stop given and determine the proper speed.

Frame 5	5′	10′

Use f/2.8 if possible. If not, use f/4.

Frame 6	5′	10′
Frame 7	5′	10′

Use f/16, if possible. If not, use f/11.

Frames 8, 9, 10: Use a row of cans, fence posts, locker handles, or other objects. Aim the camera down the row so that each object in the row can be seen in the viewfinder. Focus on the object that is about 1/3 of the way into the scene. Determine the speed.

Frame 8 — use f/2, if possible. If not, use f/2.8.
Frame 9 — use f/8.
Frame 10 — use f/16, if possible. If not use f/11.

Note: If the day you shoot is sunny and bright, take your pictures in the shade so that you can use the full range of f-stops. Then develop the film, make a contact sheet, and make a 3-1/2 x 5 in. enlargement of frames 2, 3, and 4 **or** 5, 6, and 7.

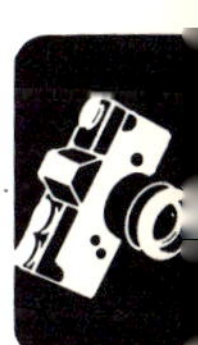

COMPOSITION

Chapter **10**

The way that subjects are arranged in a photograph is called **composition.** You must consider many factors when composing a good picture, Fig. 10-1. Your main purpose, however, is to achieve an interesting picture. Not everyone agrees on the meaning of good composition. You will develop your own style.

Good composition is not difficult to achieve. It simply takes some thought and awareness. Good composition involves the following major determinations.

1. Selection — determine the subject to be photographed.

2. Establish a center of interest. A center of interest can be established by using:
   a. color
   b. light against dark
   c. dark against light
   d. large object among small
   e. small object among large
   f. detail

3. Movement — lines or arrangement of objects causes the eyes to move to the areas the photographer wants you to see.

4. Space — the space occupied by the object and the space surrounding the object

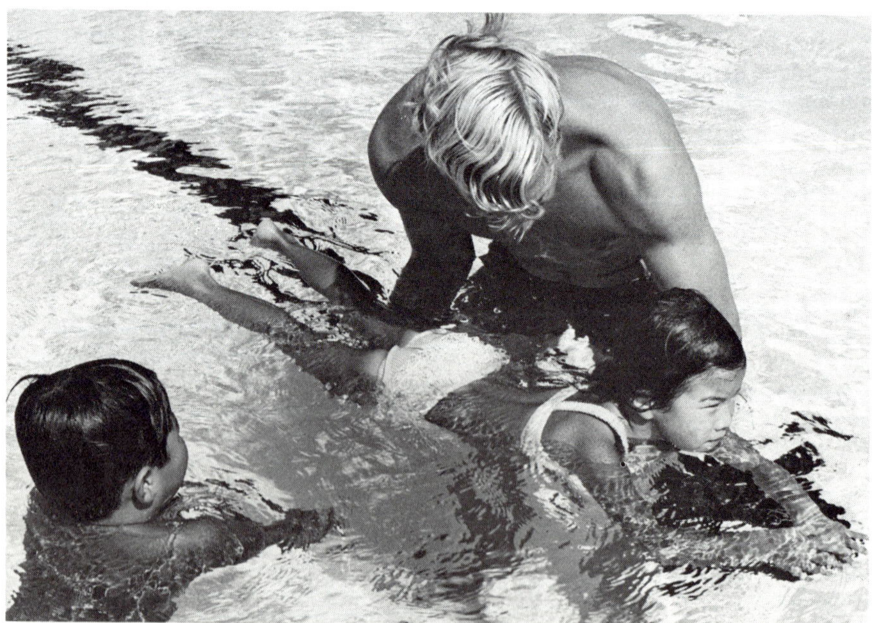

Fig. 10-1. This picture has good composition. What do you like about this picture? Would you have shot the picture differently?

become equally important. The surrounding space is called negative space. This space should not pull the viewers eye away from the subject of the photograph. The space occupied by the subject is termed positive space.

CENTER OF INTEREST

A pleasing composition has a main figure, form, or area. The other parts of the picture should not detract from the main area or object. What is the main subject of Fig. 10-2?

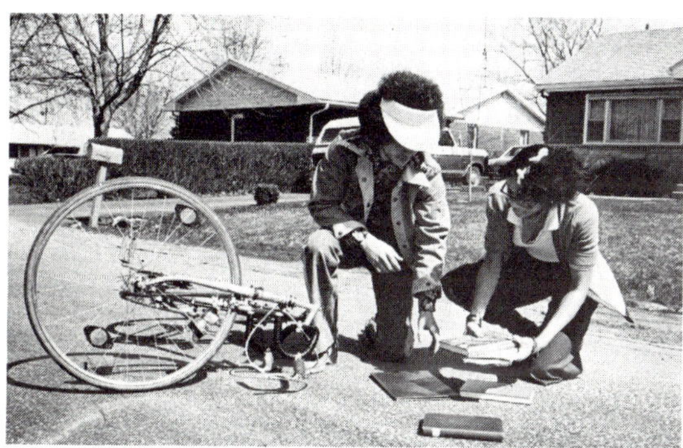

Fig. 10-2. Every picture should have a main subject or center of interest. Here, it is the two people picking up the books.

Where you place the center of interest is important to the composition of your picture. Generally, **do not** position the subject in the center of the picture. This can produce uninteresting results. Instead, place the subject off center. Use the **rule of thirds.** Imagine that the picture area is divided into thirds, both vertically and horizontally, Fig. 10-3. Place your center of interest at one of the four places where the lines cross. Have the subject look or move toward the center of the picture, Fig. 10-4.

INTERESTING ANGLES

When possible, walk around your subject and find the best angle from which to shoot the picture, Fig. 10-5. Consider the background when choosing the angle. Shooting from a low angle can give you an uncluttered sky. Suppose you do not like the background. You can consider shooting from a high angle so that only your subject and the immediate area show in the picture. Always try to choose an angle that provides an uncluttered background.

Also, consider the horizon line. Avoid locating the horizon in the middle of your picture as this cuts the picture in half. The horizon

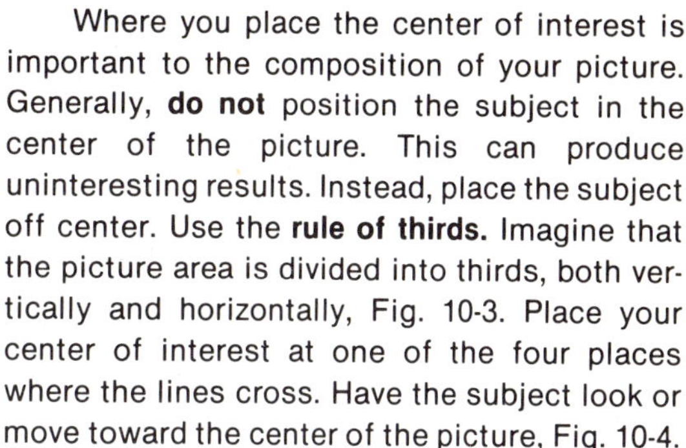

Fig. 10-3. When placing your center of interest in the picture, use the rule of thirds. Place your subject at any of the places where the lines cross.

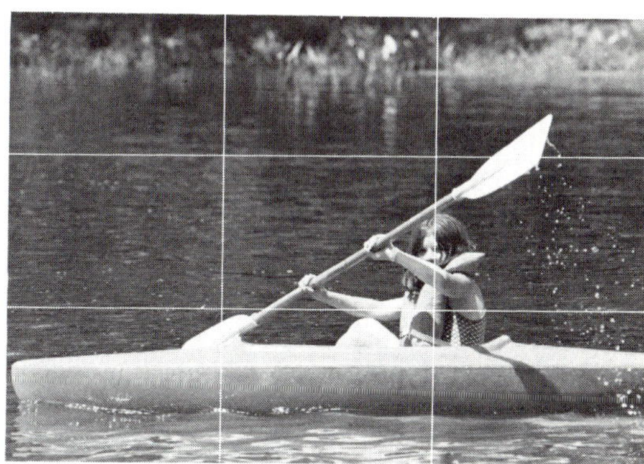

Fig. 10-4. This picture has good composition because the photographer followed the rule of thirds. Also, note that the action is moving toward the center of the picture.

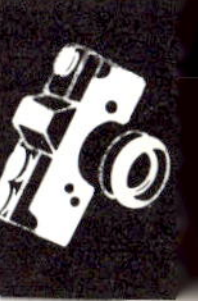

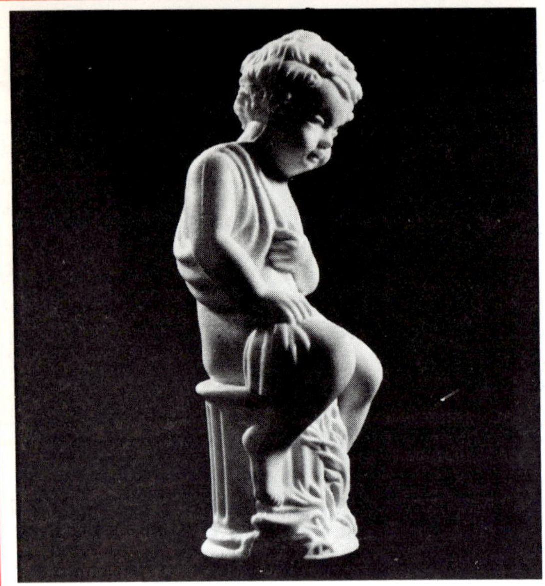

A. From left side.

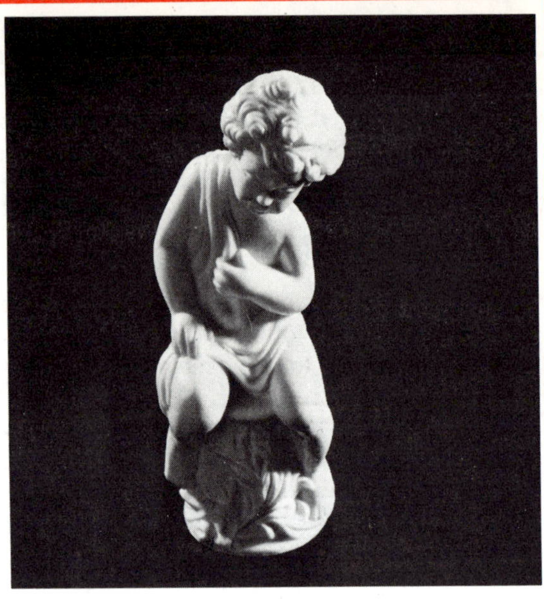

C. From above.

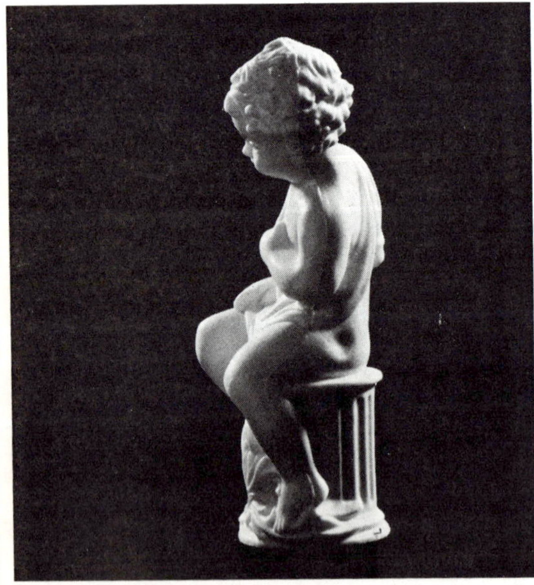

B. From right side.

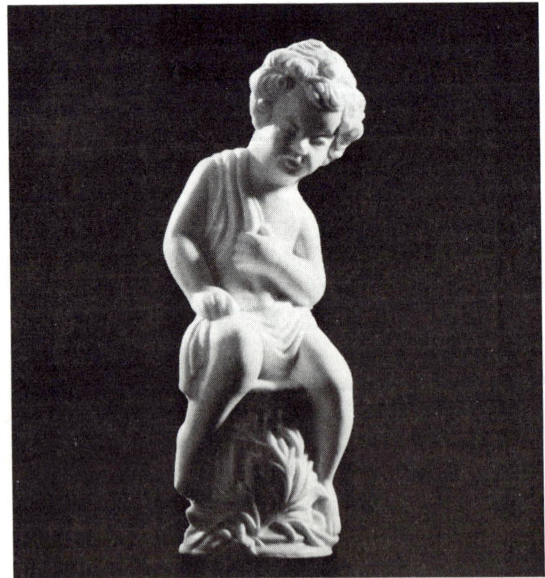

D. From below.

Fig. 10-5. Consider the possible angles from which you can shoot your picture. Which angle is best for this picture?

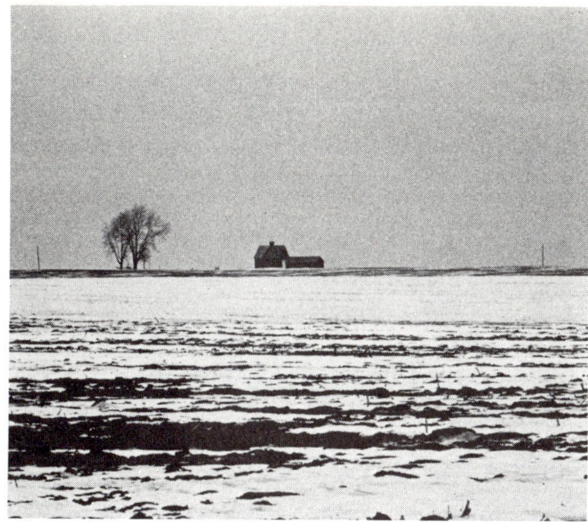 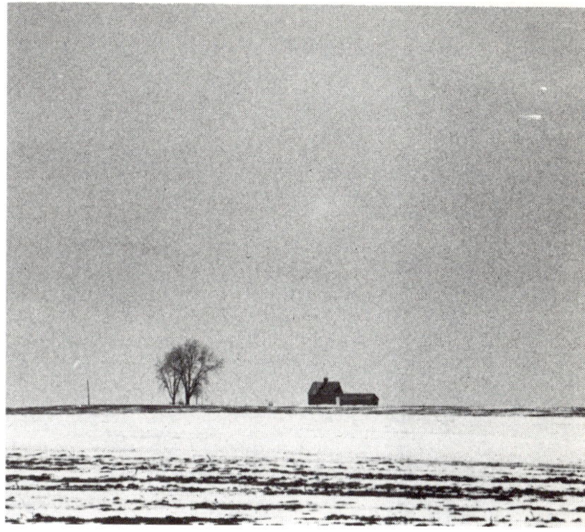

Fig. 10-6.   Either a high or low horizon line is more interesting than one that cuts the picture in half.

should be either low or high in the picture, Fig. 10-6. Once again, apply the rule of thirds. A low horizon line gives a feeling of spaciousness. A high horizon gives a feeling of closeness. Make sure, too, that the horizon is a straight line in your picture, not tipped.

MOVING IN CLOSE

Get close enough to your subject so that you can eliminate unwanted background, Fig. 10-7. Many beginning photographers do not get close enough to their subject to take the picture. Closeups give a feeling of intimacy. Long shots give a feeling of space and depth.

USING LINES FOR INTEREST AND UNITY

Lines, such as rows of trees, fences, and railroad tracks, add **perspective** (depth) to your

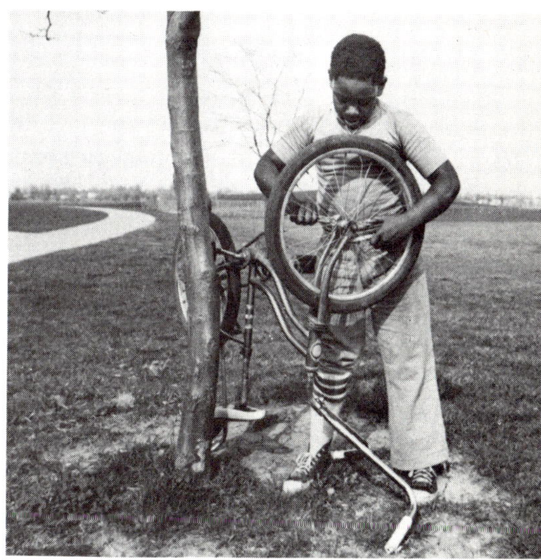

Fig. 10-7.   Get close to your subject to avoid including distracting objects or people in your picture. If this picture had been taken farther from the subject, the tree and sidewalk would have taken attention away from the subject.

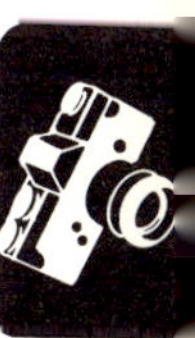

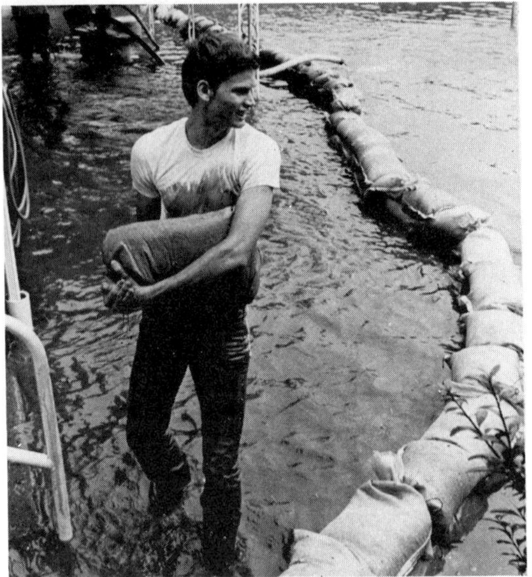

Fig. 10-8. Lines of objects can add perspective and bring unity to your picture, as sand bags do here.

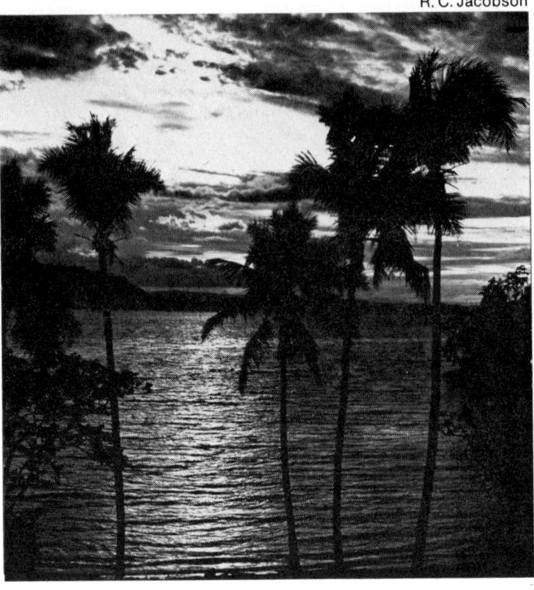

R. C. Jacobson

Fig. 10-9. Contrast is important to composition. Notice how the dark trees contrast with the clouded sky and rippling water.

pictures. Also, the lines in one object tend to unify a picture because the viewer's eyes follow the lines. Generally, lines should run into the picture rather than out of it. Often by simply changing the camera angle, you can create interesting lines in your pictures, Fig. 10-8.

USING CONTRASTS

Position light forms or colors against dark ones for contrast, Figure 10-9. Often, light striking one side of the subject (sidelighting) can add a pleasing effect, Fig. 10-10. Such contrast helps make an interesting composition.

CHOOSING THE BACKGROUND

Cluttered backgrounds ruin many pictures. Be aware of telephone poles, wires, fences, jagged shapes, and areas of bright color in the background. A good background can help set the mood of the picture and can add beauty. A cluttered background detracts from the subject, Fig. 10-11. Definite horizontal or vertical lines in the background pull the eye away from the subject. Solid or plain areas such as hedges, bushes, or a clear blue sky make good backgrounds. Remember, too, that you can blur out a poor background by controlling the depth of field.

FRAMING THE SUBJECT

Your pictures will have more interest if you **frame** the subject. For example, a baseball player sliding into base framed in the picture by the legs of another player captures attention quickly. Figure 10-12 shows how dynamic framing can be. Depth of field is also important in framing your picture. Make sure that the foreground object is in focus. Out-of-focus foreground is distracting.

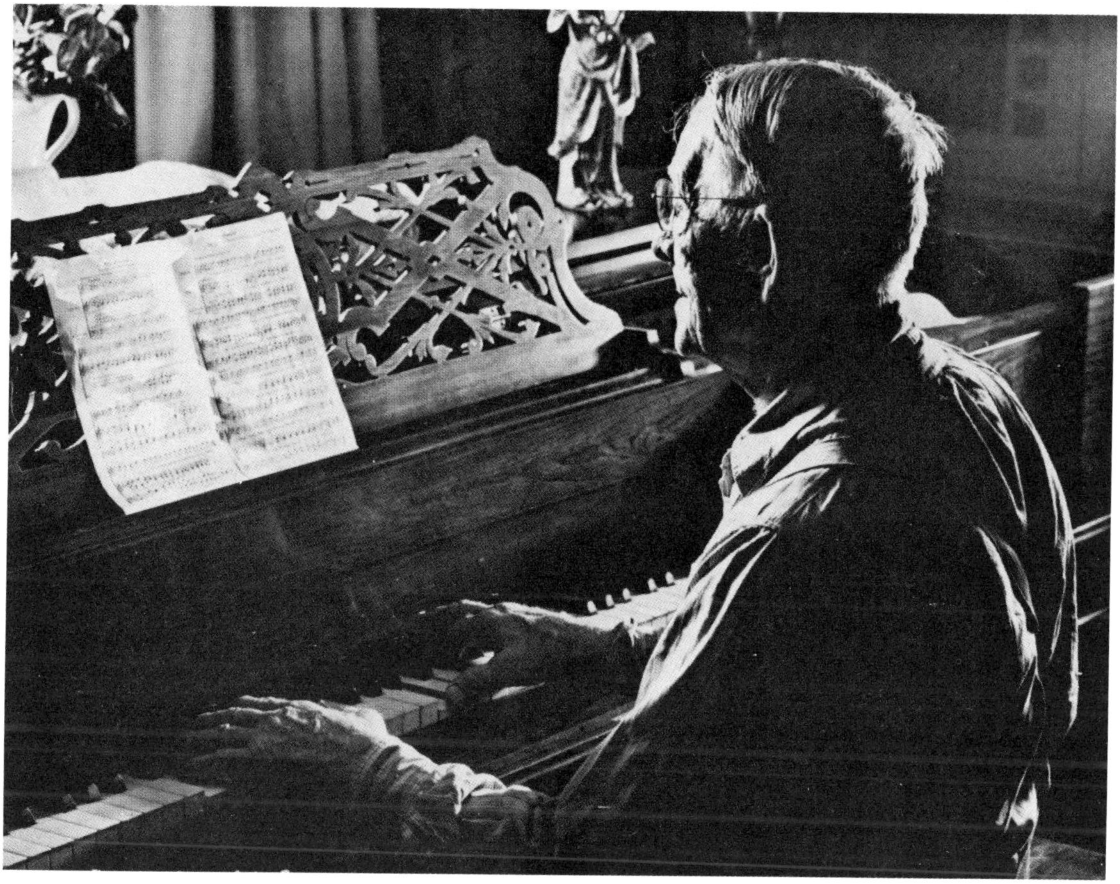

Fig. 10-10. The side and back lighting can bring out interesting contrasts.

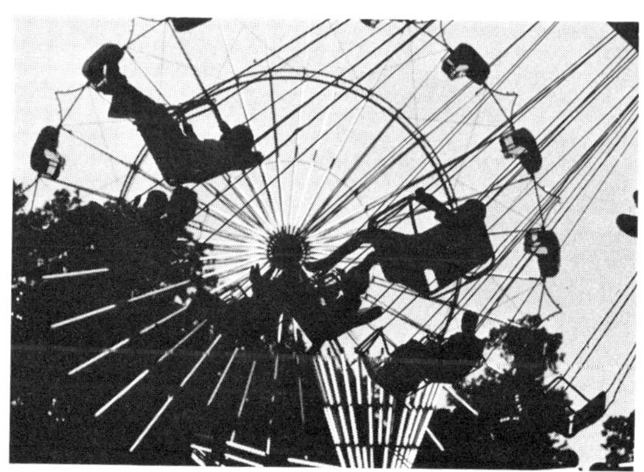

A. Cluttered background distracts from the subject.

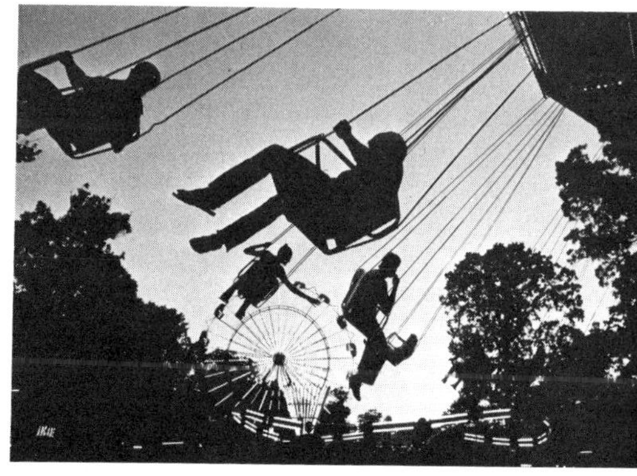

B. The right background enhances the subject.

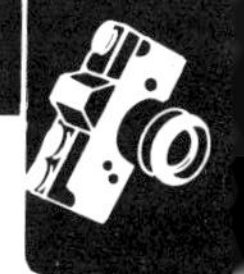

Fig. 10-11. Think about the background before you shoot.

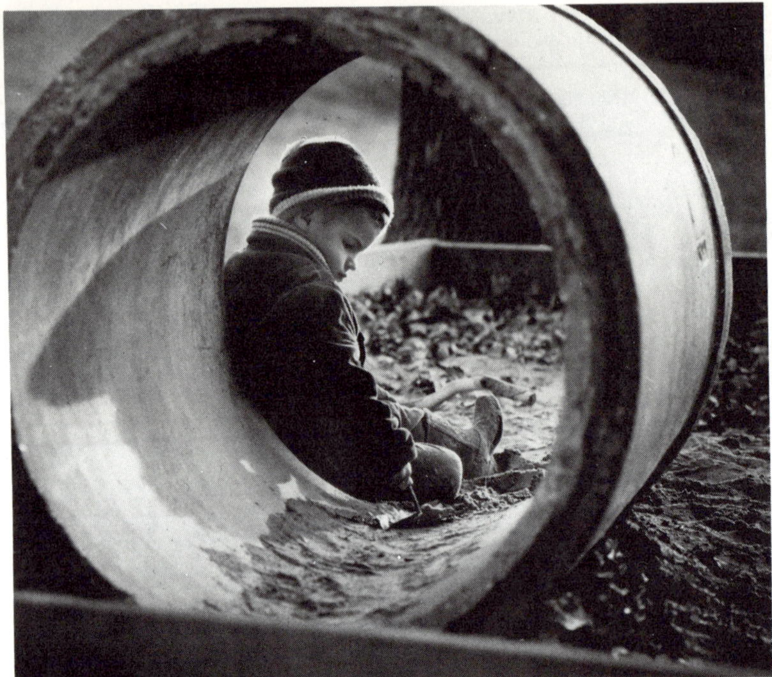

Fig. 10-12. Framing your subject can add interest and perspective. Be sure the foreground is in focus however.

Charles Raleigh

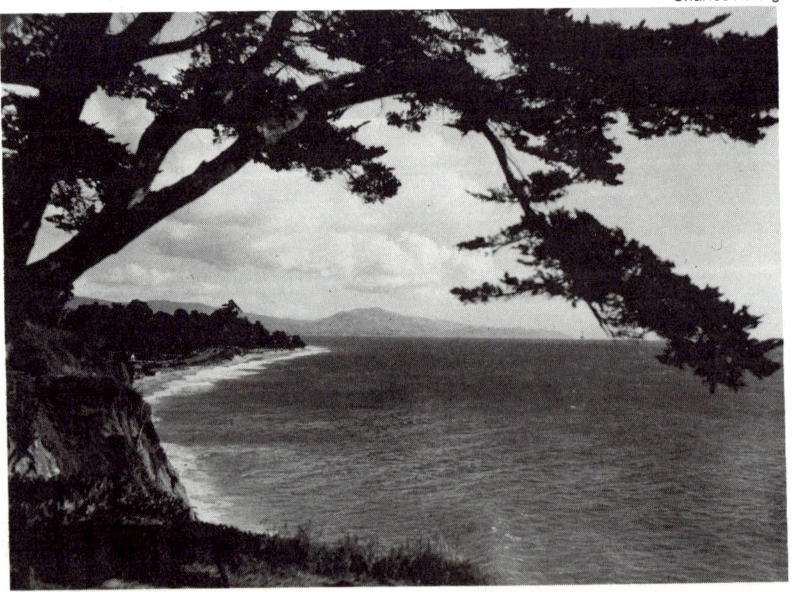

Fig. 10-13. To add depth to long shots, include objects or people in the foreground. Here, the tree adds depth to this beach scene.

ADDING DEPTH TO LONG SHOTS

Scenery shots can seem flat if there is nothing in the foreground to give the feeling of depth. See Fig. 10-13. Any people in the foreground should be looking at the scene, not at the camera. Also, they should be at least 25 feet (7.5 m) away from the camera. Long shots with interesting foregrounds require a long depth of field.

STUDY QUESTIONS

1. What is composition?
2. List the guidelines for good composition.
3. Using the rule of thirds, where should you place your main subject?
4. Explain how the horizon line can affect your pictures.
5. Why is it important to choose a good background? Give three ways that you can control the background without moving the subject.
6. Explain what is meant by framing your pictures.
7. How can you add depth to long scenery shots?

ACTIVITY 10 — COMPOSING YOUR PICTURES

Assignment

Prepare to hand in the following assignment.
1. Ten negatives from roll of Plus X film.
2. Contact sheet.
3. Photography record sheet.

Materials Needed

Plus X film
1 sheet 5 x 7 in. polycontrast F paper
Darkroom supplies

Frame 1: Take a picture of your name, hour, and assignment in the same manner as previous activities.

Frames 2-10: Shoot pictures as specified below, using any order you wish. Be sure to note on your photo record sheet the purpose for each frame.

1. A picture in which there is high contrast between the subject and other objects in the picture.
2. A shot in which there is a fairly straight horizon line or ground line.
3. A shot taken from a high angle looking down on your subject or from a low angle looking up at it.
4. A picture having a strong line or lines.
5. A picture which is framed by a foreground object.
6. A long shot (scenery) with a person or object in the foreground to add depth.
7. A closeup of an object.
8. A shot with a good background.
9. A shot of your choice to show good composition.

Developing and Printing

1. Develop your film.
2. Make a contact print of your negatives.

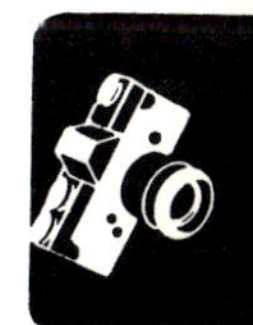

TAKING ACTION PICTURES   Chapter **11**

An action picture is one in which the movement of the subject is stopped. Movement is not blurred. Most sports pictures are action shots, Figure 11-1. Action can be stopped in two ways:

1. Use a fast shutter speed.
2. Pan the camera.

When a fast shutter speed is used, the camera remains stationary. When the camera is panned, it is moved with subject and the picture is shot during this movement. See Fig. 11-2.

FAST SHUTTER SPEED

Fast shutter speeds are those at 1/250, 1/500 or 1/1000 of a second. Both the subject and the background will be sharp and clear as you can see in view **A** of Fig. 11-2.

You must consider several factors when taking action shots. First, the **closer** you are to the moving subject, the **faster** the shutter speed you will need. For example, if you were 10 feet or 3-1/2 meters away from a moving object, you

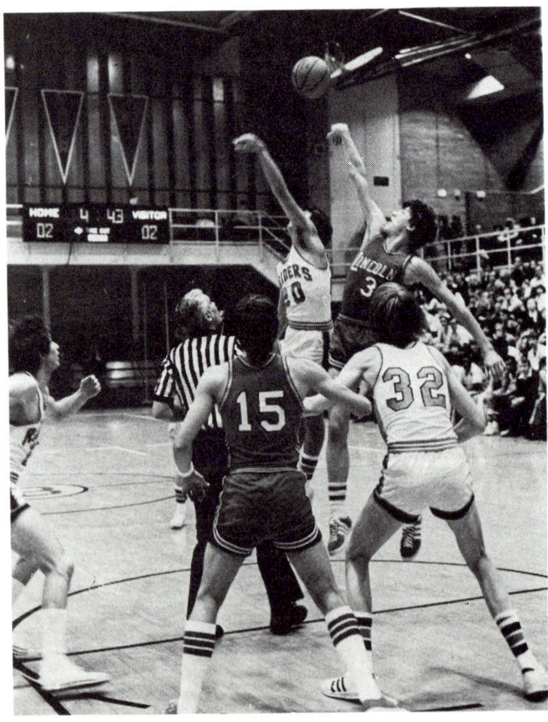

Fig. 11-1. Action shots challenge the skills of the photographer.

would use a faster shutter speed than if you were 100 feet or 30-1/2 meters away. In Fig. 11-3, note the difference in sharpness of the subject taken at two different distances at the same shutter speed. A faster shutter speed is needed in view A to improve the sharpness of the subject.

Secondly, subjects moving at right angles to the camera require a faster shutter speed than those moving directly toward or away from

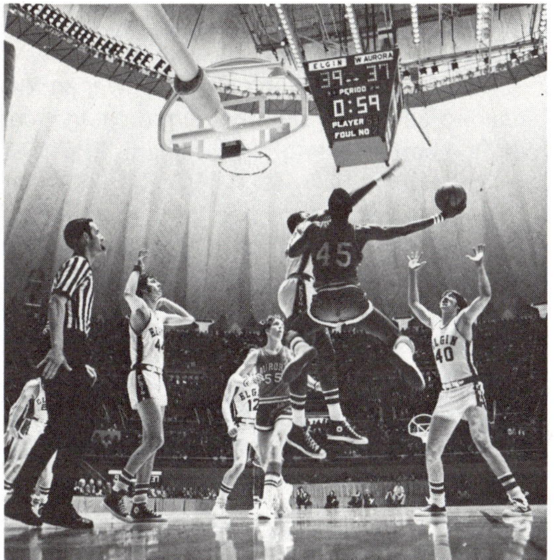

A. Using a fast shutter speed.

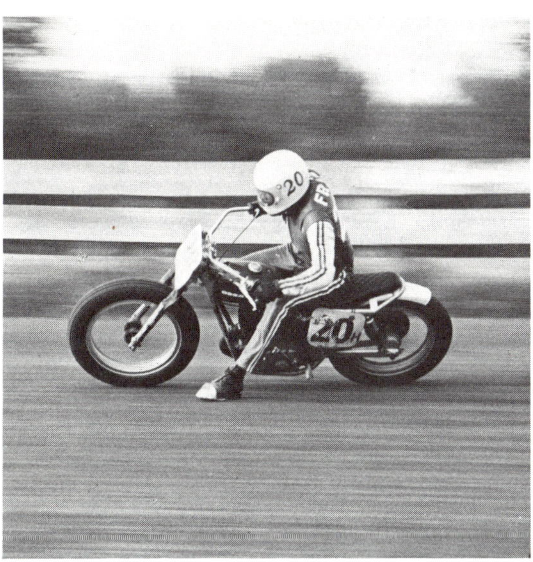

B. Panning the camera.

Fig. 11-2. Using a fast shutter speed or panning the subject can stop the action. Notice the difference in the backgrounds.

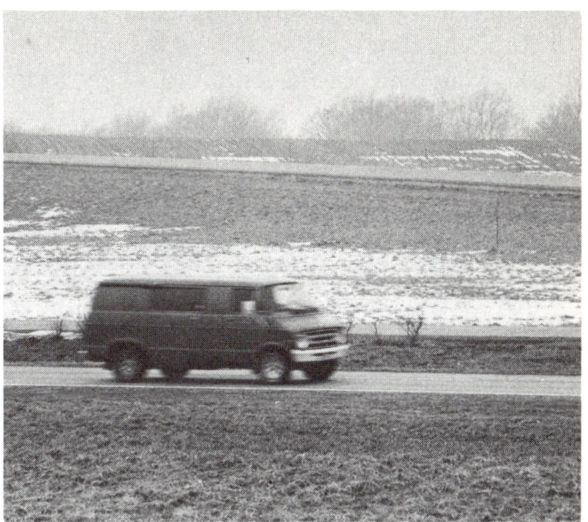

A. Shutter speed too slow for closeup of action.

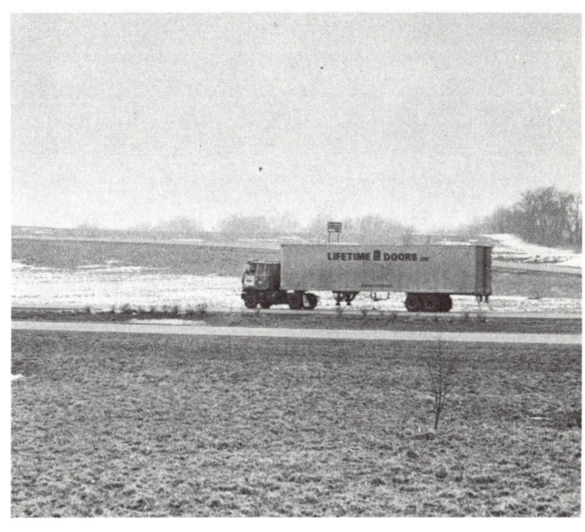

B. Shutter speed fast enough for a long shot of action.

Fig. 11-3. The closeup of a moving subject requires a faster shutter speed than a subject farther away. Both of these pictures were taken at 1/125 of a second, but note the difference in sharpness of the subject.

the camera. See Fig. 11-4. Note also Fig. 11-5 which shows how shutter speed relates to distance and camera angle. Study it carefully so that you understand how to use shutter speed to best advantage.

Certain types of action have a peak or pause in them when action almost stops. For example, for a high jumper the peak is at the top of the jump. For a golfer it is at the top of the back-swing, and for a diver at the height of the dive. Action is easier to stop if you shoot the picture at this peak, because for a split second the subject is not moving. A slower shutter speed can be used if you catch the action during this slight pause.

Shutter speed can help you be creative in your action shots. Often using a slower shutter speed to achieve a slightly blurred subject can create a better feeling of movement, Fig. 11-6.

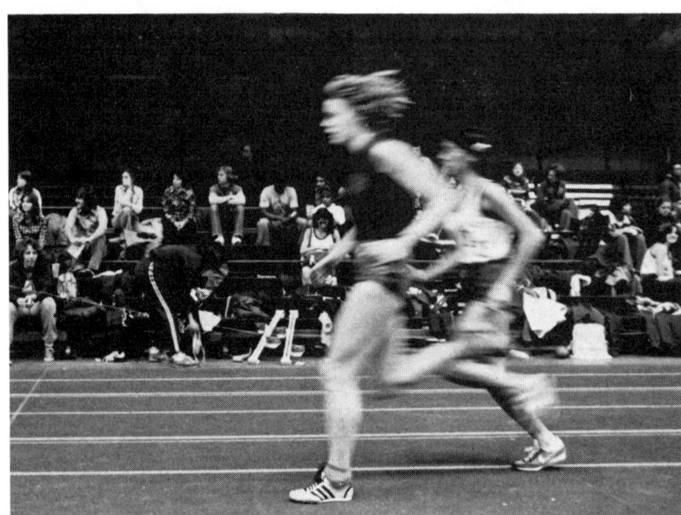

Fig. 11-4. A subject moving at right angles to the subject requires a faster shutter speed than one moving toward or away from the camera.

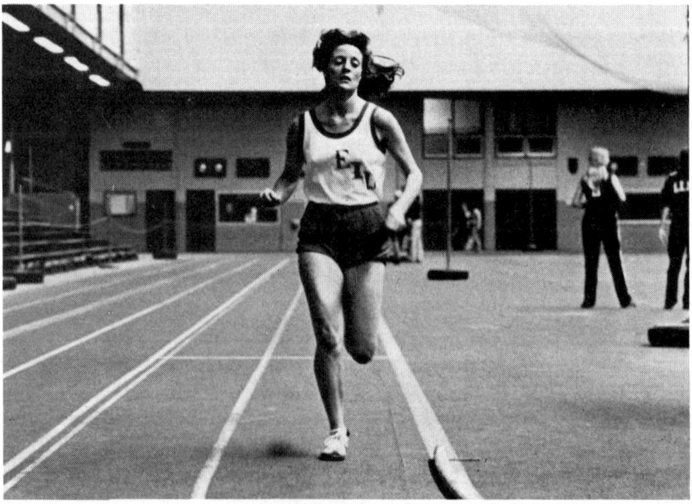

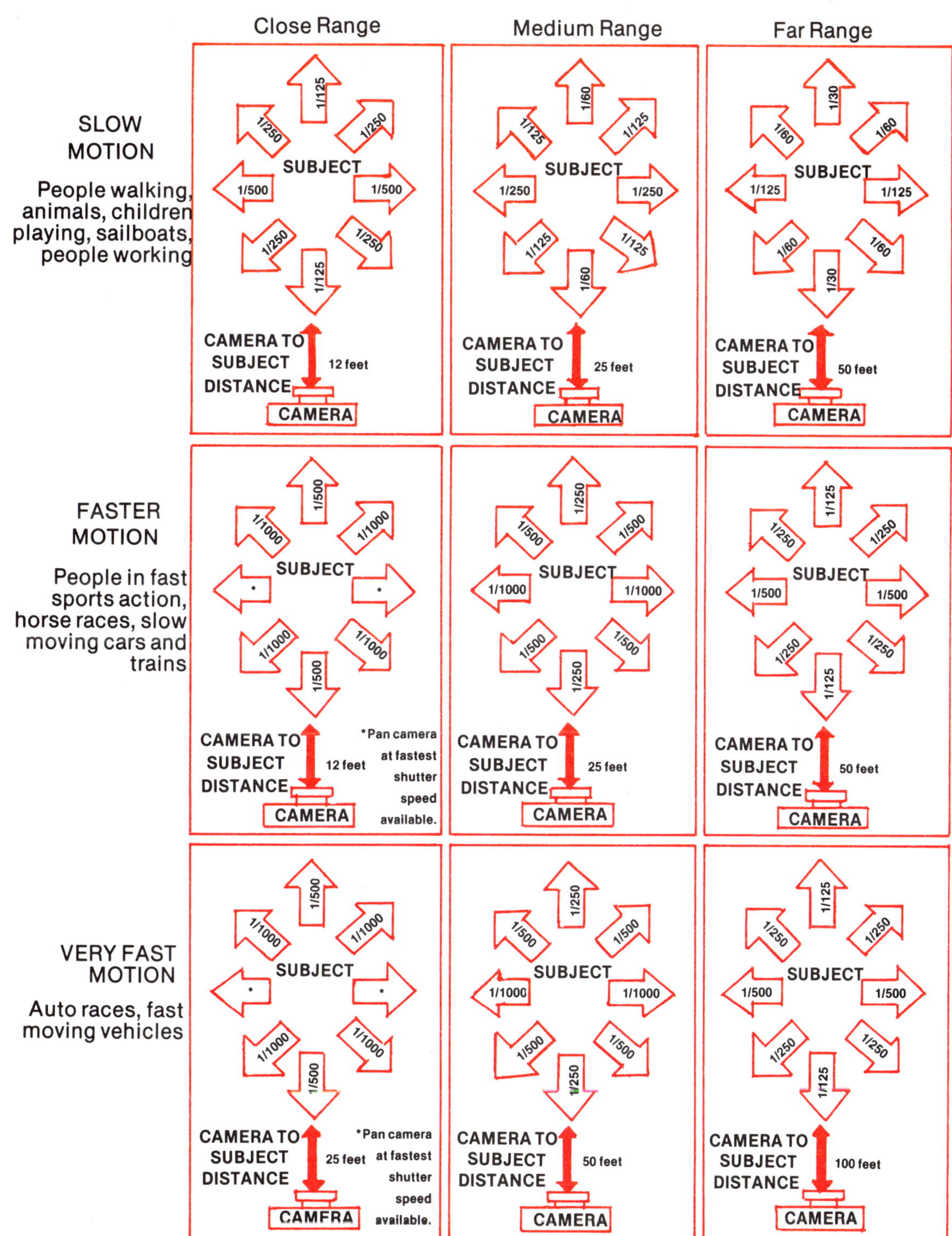

Fig. 11-5.
Shutter Speeds for Action Pictures
Arrows indicate direction of motion

Close Range
Medium Range
Far Range

SLOW MOTION

People walking, animals, children playing, sailboats, people working

1/125
1/250
1/250
1/500
1/500
1/250
1/250
1/125
SUBJECT
CAMERA TO SUBJECT DISTANCE
12 feet
CAMERA

1/60
1/125
1/125
1/250
1/250
1/125
1/125
1/60
SUBJECT
CAMERA TO SUBJECT DISTANCE
25 feet
CAMERA

1/30
1/60
1/60
1/125
1/125
1/60
1/60
1/30
SUBJECT
CAMERA TO SUBJECT DISTANCE
50 feet
CAMERA

FASTER MOTION

People in fast sports action, horse races, slow moving cars and trains

1/500
1/1000
1/1000
*
*
1/1000
1/1000
1/500
SUBJECT
CAMERA TO SUBJECT DISTANCE
12 feet
CAMERA
*Pan camera at fastest shutter speed available.

1/250
1/500
1/500
1/1000
1/1000
1/500
1/500
1/250
SUBJECT
CAMERA TO SUBJECT DISTANCE
25 feet
CAMERA

1/125
1/250
1/250
1/500
1/500
1/250
1/250
1/125
SUBJECT
CAMERA TO SUBJECT DISTANCE
50 feet
CAMERA

VERY FAST MOTION

Auto races, fast moving vehicles

1/500
1/1000
1/1000
*
*
1/1000
1/1000
1/500
SUBJECT
CAMERA TO SUBJECT DISTANCE
25 feet
CAMERA
*Pan camera at fastest shutter speed available.

1/250
1/500
1/500
1/1000
1/1000
1/500
1/500
1/250
SUBJECT
CAMERA TO SUBJECT DISTANCE
50 feet
CAMERA

1/125
1/250
1/250
1/500
1/500
1/250
1/250
1/125
SUBJECT
CAMERA TO SUBJECT DISTANCE
100 feet
CAMERA

PANNING THE CAMERA

Action can also be stopped by moving the camera with the subject in motion. To do this, you must keep the subject in the viewfinder as you squeeze the shutter release. This method of shooting action blurs the background and creates a feeling of speed. See Fig. 11-7.

Panning is often a good choice for action taking place in less light than is required for fast shutter speeds. Aperture can be opened up to let in available light and the shutter speed slowed down when you pan under these conditions.

Since action shots require a fast shutter speed, what happens to the depth of field? It gets shorter. You should now understand the relationship of aperture and shutter speed. Also, you should know how each affects depth of field and motions.

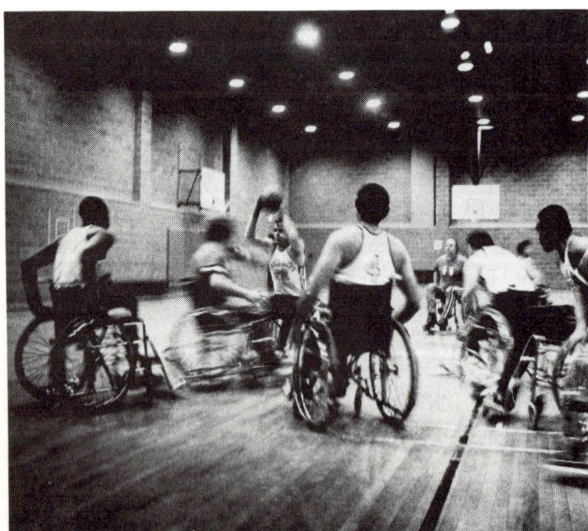

Fig. 11-6. Motion can be given a special effect when the shutter speed is slow enough to blur the subject slightly.

STUDY QUESTIONS

1. In what two ways can you stop the action if your subject is moving?
2. If you are close to your moving subject, should your shutter speed be faster or slower than if you were far away?
3. Explain how the direction the subject is moving relates to the shutter speed you need to stop the action.
4. In what kind of situation would you want your moving subject to look slightly blurred?
5. Why can you not use a fast shutter speed where little light is available?
6. Since action shots require a fast shutter speed, what happens to depth of field? Does this make careful focusing more or less important?

ACTIVITY 11 — TAKING ACTION SHOTS

Assignment

Prepare to hand in the following assignment.
1. 10 negatives from Plus X film.
2. Contact sheet.
3. One 3-1/2 x 5 in. enlargement of your best picture from frames 2-8.
4. One 3-1/2 x 5 in. enlargement from frames 9 or 10. Statement of the reasons you chose that picture for enlargement.
5. Photography record sheet.

Materials Needed

Plus X Film
4 sheets 5 x 7 in. polycontrast F paper
Darkroom supplies

Procedure

Shoot the type of picture described for each of your 10 frames. All speeds are based on a distance of no more than 25 feet.

Frame 1: Your name, hour, and activity number.

Frame 2: 1/125. Pan a fast moving object at right angles so that the background will be blurred, but the object will be sharp.

Frame 3: 1/125. Shoot a fast moving object at right angles by holding the camera still so that the object will be blurred, but the background sharp.

Frame 4: 1/60. Pan a fast moving object at right angles so that the background will be blurred and the object slightly blurred.

For **frames 5-10,** refer to Fig. 11-5 to determine the proper speeds to use. In **frames 5-8,** use a shutter speed that is only fast enough to stop the action without panning.

Frame 5: Shoot an object that is moving at right angles to you.

Frame 6: Shoot the same object moving at a diagonal to you.

Frame 7: Shoot the same object moving directly towards **or** directly away from you.

Frame 8: Throw an object in the air at close range and take a picture at a slow shutter speed as the object reaches its highest point. The object should appear motionless in this picture.

Frames 9-10: Pictures you choose to take for these two frames should emphasize the feeling of motion. Be creative, but stay simple.

Developing and Printing

1. Develop your roll of film
2. Make a contact print
3. Make a 3-1/2″ x 5″ enlargement of your best picture from frames 2-8.
4. Make a 3-1/2″ x 5″ enlargement from the picture of your choice from frames 9 and 10. Describe this picture on a separate sheet and tell why you chose it for an enlargement.

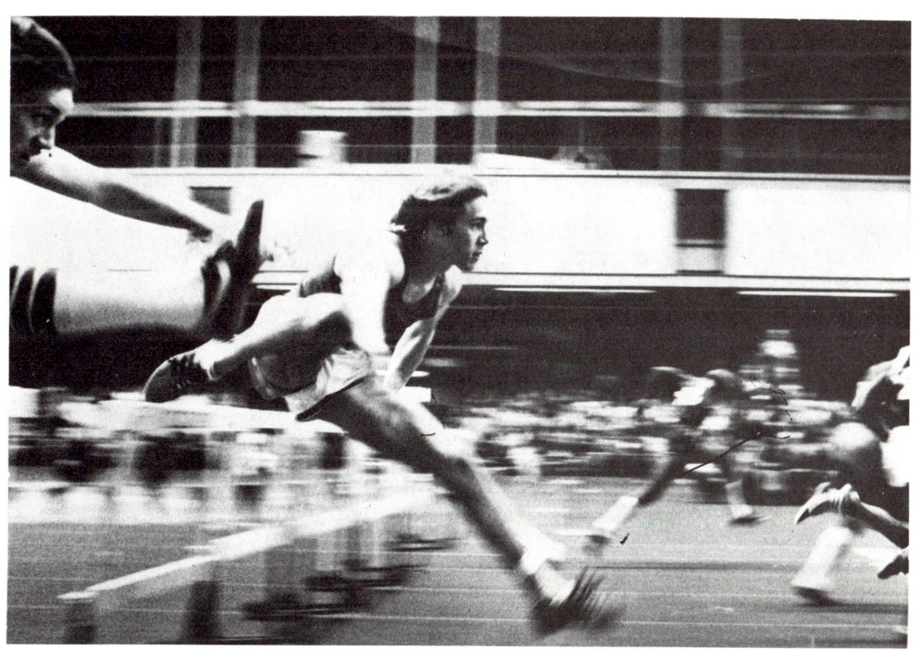
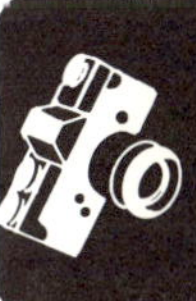

Fig. 11-7. Panning with the subject in motion creates a feeling of speed.

TAKING FLASH PICTURES

Chapter **12**

Shooting pictures at night or indoors usually requires the use of a flash, Fig. 12-1. There are different types of flash devices. Flashbulbs, flashcubes, and electronic flash are the most common, Fig. 12-2. The manual for your camera will tell you what type to use. Flash pictures can be taken at distances of 30 feet or less. Most flash devices are not powerful enough to give off enough light to photograph a far away subject.

DETERMINING THE F-STOP

Using the proper f-stop is important to good flash photography. Generally, the closer you are to the subject the smaller the aperture must be. The farther away you are, the larger the aperture must be. For example, if your subject were 4 feet or 1.2 meters away, you might use a setting of f/16. However, if you were 15 feet or 4.6 meters away you would use a setting of f/5.6.

ELECTRONIC FLASH

Electronic flash devices have a **calculator dial** on them to help you figure the f-stop. Figure 12-3 shows an electronic flash calculator dial. Notice these three readings:

1. The film ASA rating.
2. The distance.
3. The f-stop.

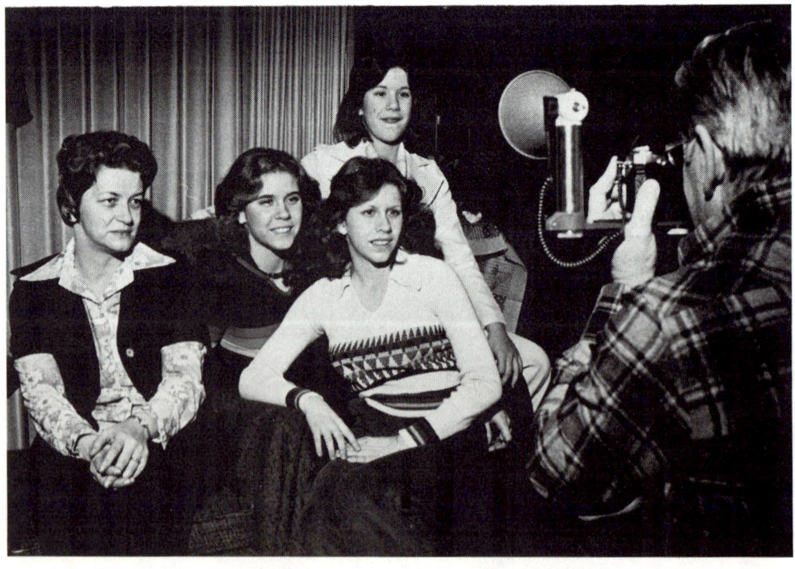

Fig. 12-1. A flash provides the extra lighting needed for pictures taken indoors.

When using an electronic flash, first set the dial to the ASA rating of the film being used. Remember that ASA pertains to the light sensitivity of the film. Next, focus your camera on the subject and determine the distance. Look at this distance on the calculator dial, noting the proper f-stop that appears just below it. Adjust your camera to this f-stop. To practice making this adjustment, determine the f-stops in the problems shown in Fig. 12-4. Work the problems based on distances shown in either U.S. customary or SI metric measurements.

FLASHBULBS

If you are using flashbulbs, you can figure the f-stop by following a **guide number.** The guide number you use depends on the type of flash device and film used. The manuals for your camera and flash device often show guide numbers. Also, film is packed with an information sheet that shows guide numbers, Fig. 12-5.

To find the correct exposure, divide the distance from flash to subject into the guide number. The formula is expressed as follows:

$$\text{f-stop} = \frac{\text{guide number}}{\text{distance}}$$

For example, if the guide number is 61 and the distance is 10 feet, you would figure the f-stop like this:

$$\text{f-stop} = \frac{61}{10} = 6.1$$

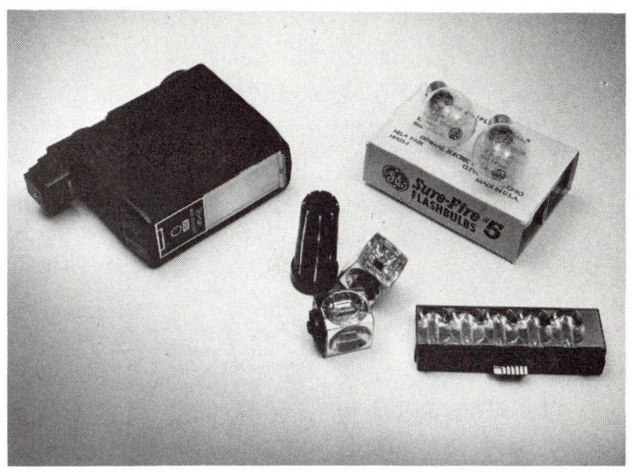

Fig. 12-2. Different types of flash devices are used on different cameras.

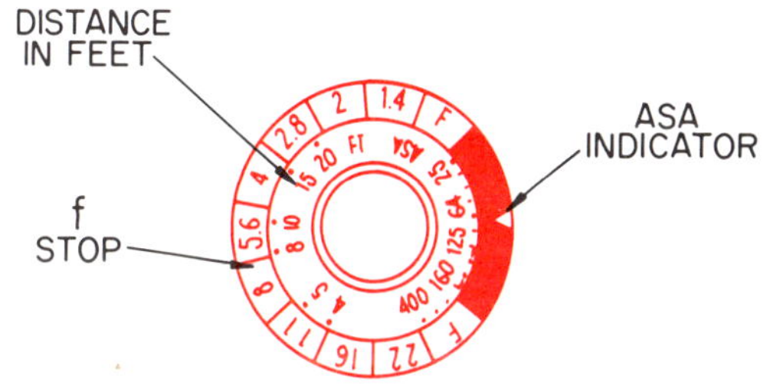

U.S. Customary	SI Equivalent
4 ft.	1.2 m
5 ft.	1.5 m
8 ft.	2.4 m
10 ft.	3 m
15 ft.	4.5 m
20 ft.	6 m

Fig. 12-3. The calculator dial on an electronic flash can help you determine the proper f-stop for flash pictures. Notice that the f-stop depends on the distance to the subject and the film's ASA rating.

<table>
<tr><td colspan="2">U.S. Customary Measurements</td><td colspan="2">SI Metric Measurements</td></tr>
<tr><td>Distance = 10′</td><td>f-stop = ______</td><td>Distance = 3 m</td><td>f-stop = ______</td></tr>
<tr><td>Distance = 5′</td><td>f-stop = ______</td><td>Distance = 1.5 m</td><td>f-stop = ______</td></tr>
<tr><td>Distance = 15′</td><td>f-stop = ______</td><td>Distance = 4.5 m</td><td>f-stop = ______</td></tr>
<tr><td>Distance = 20′</td><td>f-stop = ______</td><td>Distance = 6 m</td><td>f-stop = ______</td></tr>
</table>

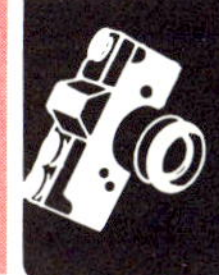

Fig. 12-4. Answers: To come from art.

The closest f-stop to 6.1 is 5.6. Therefore, f/5.6 is the setting you would use.

Before taking flash pictures, be sure you know the guide number for the film and flash device you are using. Otherwise, your pictures will be overexposed or underexposed. Figure 12-6 shows an underexposed picture.

FLASH CUBES AND FLASH BARS

Flash cubes and flash bars are commonly used with instamatic cameras. A few models also have built-in or separate electronic flash devices. In most cases, artificial light sources of this type have a limit range. The maximum distance between camera and subject should not exceed 15 feet (4.65 m). The next time you are at a stadium or graduation see how many people break this rule. These photographers waste a great deal of money when they use their flash in this manner.

SHUTTER SPEED

Usually, the shutter speed to use with flash is determined by the type of camera you are using. Your camera manual tells you the speed to use for flash pictures. If you try to shoot at a faster speed than is correct, the shutter will close before all of the film for that frame is exposed, as shown in Fig. 12-6. Generally, a slow shutter speed such as 1/30 is required. At a slow shutter speed, the shutter will be open when the flash goes off. This is called **synchronization.** The flash lasts a very short time — often less than 1/2000 of a second. On the other hand, if the flash goes off before or after the shutter has opened, no light gets to the film. The faster the shutter speed, the greater the chance that the shutter will be closed when the flash goes off. The shutter speed dial on your camera should tell the speed to use for flash. Some cameras allow you to shoot at a faster speed, such as 1/60 or 1/125 of a second. Taking good pictures depends upon your knowledge of your camera.

FLASH PICTURES

BLUE FLASHBULBS: Determine f-number for average subjects by dividing guide number for reflector and flashbulb by distance in feet from flash to subject. If negatives are consistently too light, increase exposure by using lower guide number; if too dark, reduce exposure by using higher guide number.

GUIDE NUMBERS FOR BLUE FLASHBULBS						
Type of Reflector	**Flashbulb**	**Shutter Speed**				
		X Sync	**M Synchronization**			
		1/30	1/30	1/60	1/125	1/250
	Flashcube	100	70	65	55	44
	Hi-Power Flashcube	140	90	90	80	65
	AG-1B	75	50	50	42	36
	AG-1B	100	70	70	60	50
	M2B	100	NR	NR	NR	NR
*	AG-1B	150	100	100	85	70
	M2B	130	NR	NR	NR	NR
	M3B, 5B, 25B	140	130	120	100	85
	6B†, 26B†	NR	140	100	70	50
*	M3B, 5B, 25B	200	180	180	150	120
	6B†, 26B†	NR	200	140	100	70

*Polished bowl.   †Bulbs for focal-plane shutter.   NR—Not Recommended.

Caution: Bulbs may shatter when flashed; use a flashguard over your reflector. Do not use flash in an explosive atmosphere. See flashbulb manufacturer's instructions.

Fig. 12-5. Every roll of film has a fact sheet that gives flash guide numbers for determining f-stop.

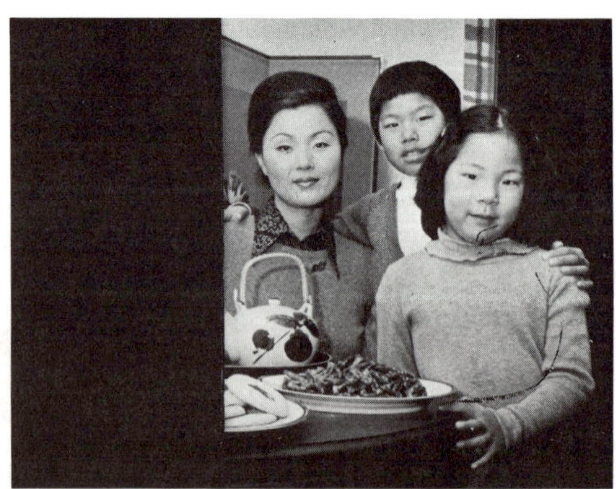

Fig. 12-6. This flash picture was shot at too fast a shutter speed, resulting in a large amount of black area.

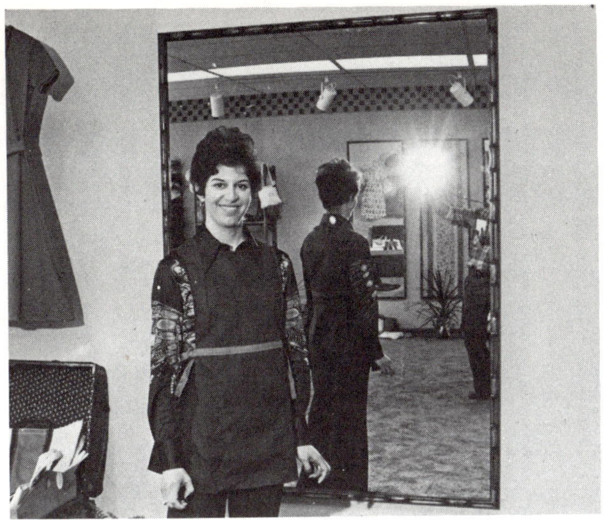

A. Shooting directly toward a reflective surface.

Fig. 12-7. Avoid flash reflections. When the background is reflective, shoot at an angle.

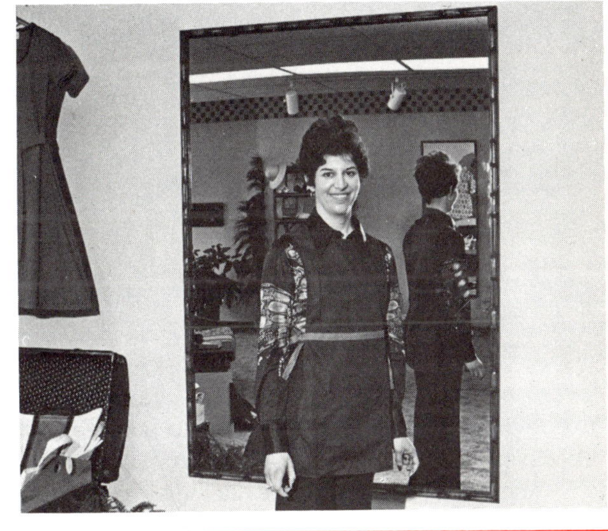

B. Shoot at an angle.

POINTERS FOR USING FLASH

Mirrors and windows can cause reflections in flash pictures. Therefore, avoid aiming directly into mirrors or windows. The flash will reflect back to the camera and spoil your picture. See Fig. 12-7. If you must use flash near a reflecting surface, take the picture at an angle, as shown in view **B.**

Size of room and color of walls help determine the aperture to be used. If you are shooting in a small room with light colored walls and ceiling, close down one f-stop because more light will be reflected. If you are shooting in a very large room such as a gym or outdoors at night, open up one or two f-stops, depending upon the distance to the subject.

Often a flash gives the subject a harsh, flat look. The subject's appearance can be softened by placing one or two layers of white handkerchief over the flash, Fig. 12-8. Open up one f-stop for each layer of handkerchief. Usually,

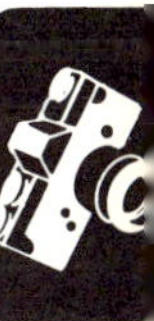

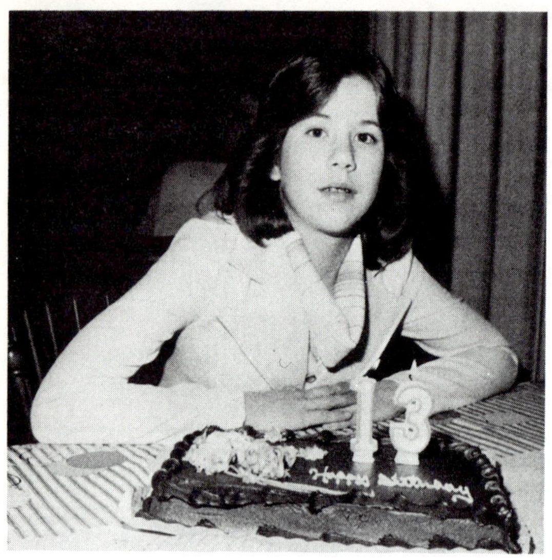

A. Using straight flash.

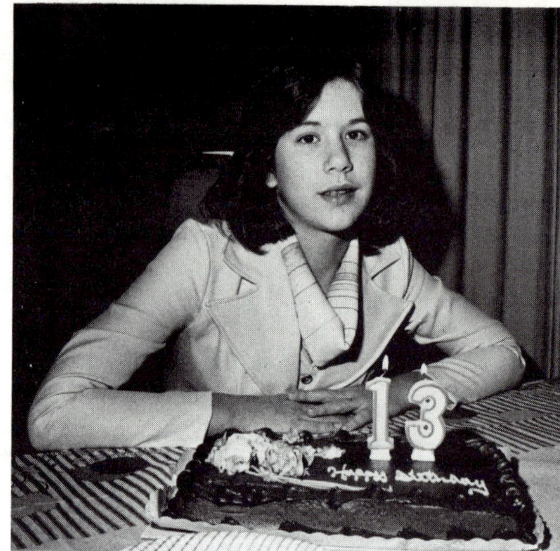

B. Using two layers of white handkerchief.

Fig. 12-8. Using one or two layers of white handkerchief over a flash can soften the flat look. Open one f-stop for each layer of handkerchief.

two layers at the most are enough to achieve success.

Another way to get a more realistic looking flash picture is to **bounce** the flash, Fig. 12-9. This softens the harsh flash and helps avoid shadows. In this procedure, you must remove the flash device or tilt it up from the camera and aim it at the ceiling, walls or a sheet. The light is reflected from this surface onto the subject. The f-stop must be opened one or two stops to bounce the flash.

When taking flash pictures of a group of people, be sure they are all about an **equal distance** from the flash. Otherwise, the close people will be overexposed and those far away underexposed, Figure 12-10.

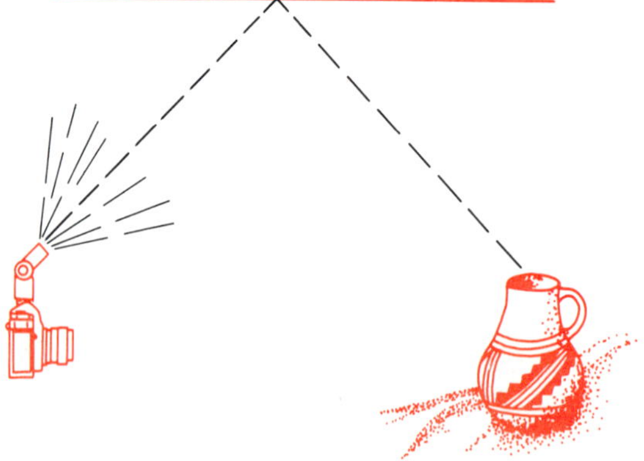

Fig. 12-9. Bouncing the flash off a light ceiling gives indoor pictures a soft, realistic appearance. Open up one or two f-stops to bounce the flash.

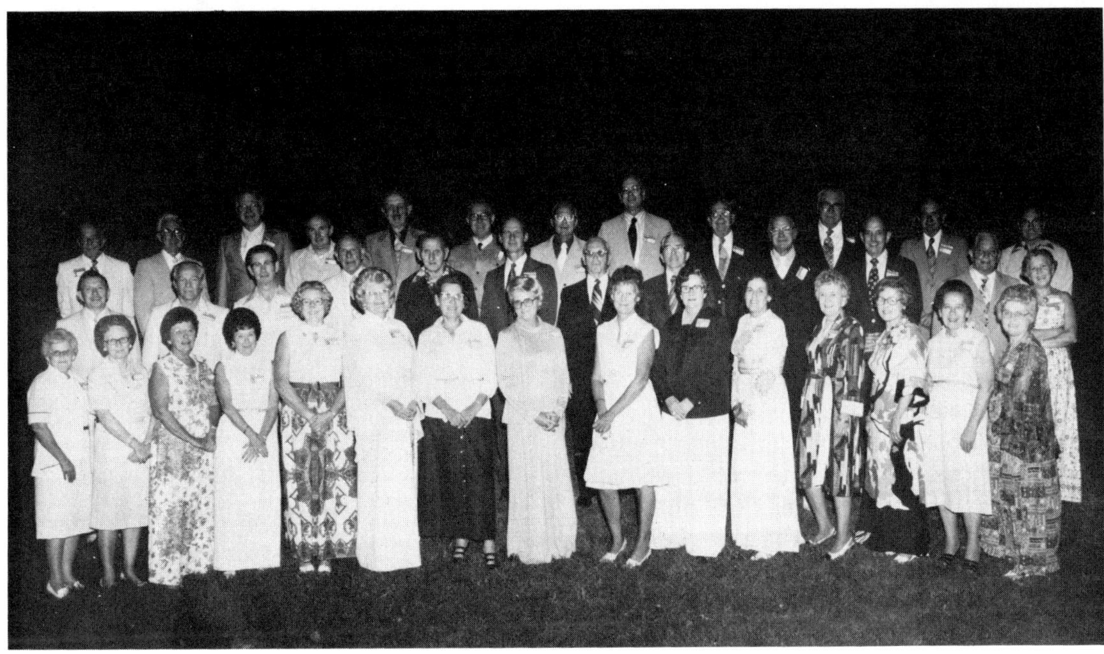

Fig. 12-10. Arranging people in this group at about equal distance from the flash would have resulted in a far better picture.

STUDY QUESTIONS

1. What is the maximum distance at which a flash is usually effective?
2. Explain how f-stop relates to distance from the subject when flash is used.
3. What three factors are involved in a flash calculator?
4. Briefly explain how to use guide numbers. Where do you find the guide numbers for the film and flash you are using?
5. Why is shutter speed important when taking flash pictures?
6. How do mirrors and windows affect flash pictures?
7. Explain two ways to cut down on the harsh, flat look of a flash picture.

ACTIVITY — 12
TAKING FLASH PICTURES

Assignment

Prepare to hand in the following assignment.
1. Ten negatives from a roll of Plus X film.
2. Contact sheet.
3. One 5″ x 7″ enlargement of your best shot.
4. Photography record sheet.

Materials Needed

35 mm Plus X film
4 sheets 5″ x 7″ polycontrast F paper
35 mm camera and flash device
Darkroom supplies

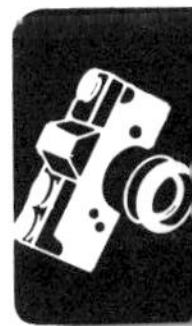

Procedure

Take the following pictures indoors using flash. After the first frame, you may shoot these in any order.

Frame 1: Your name, hour, and activity number.

Frame 2: Depth of field shot — (row of cans, lockers, etc.)

Frame 3: Portrait of a person or object using a straight flash.

Frame 4: Same as frame 3, but use a bounce flash.

Frame 5: Close action shot in a gym or other indoor area.

Frame 6: Closeup of a still life using a handkerchief over the flash to cut down light. (Open one f-stop for one layer of handkerchief.) The still life can be a stack of books, arrangement of objects, or any other choice of subject. Be creative.

Frame 7: Fast movement, such as a ball dropping which you stop by flash. Shoot in a dimly lighted room so that existing light does not cause the object to be blurred. Get close to the object.

Frame 8: Object or person in front of a glass door or highly reflective wall, using direct flash. This is to show the effect of flash reflection.

Frame 9: Same subject as frame 7, but shoot at an angle to avoid reflection.

Frame 10: Your choice of subject shot at one shutter speed faster than the camera is designed for flash pictures. This is to show how only part of the picture will receive the necessary light.

Developing and Printing

1. Develop your film.
2. Make a contact print.
3. Choose your best picture and make a 5″ x 7″ enlargement.

ADVANCED DARKROOM PROCEDURES

Chapter 13

Darkroom techniques have an important part in greatly improving many pictures. With their use, light can be controlled in enlargements to create special effects. Overexposed or underexposed portions of negatives can be corrected when making prints. Unwanted parts of a picture can be eliminated in the final print. Details can be softened. These and other ways to improve pictures or create special effects through darkroom procedures are discussed in this chapter.

CROPPING

Often, a picture shows more detail than necessary to be interesting. In fact, the extra details may detract from the subject. This may occur because the photographer was not or could not get close to the subject. The unwanted details can be omitted by blocking them out during printing. This is called **cropping,** Fig. 13-1.

First, make an enlargement of the entire negative so that details of the picture can be studied. Cut two L-shaped pieces of cardboard and use them to frame the details you want to include, Fig. 13-2. Use the cardboard as a mask to move back and forth over the test print, adjusting its size to find the part of your picture that has the best composition. Mark this area with a heavy pencil so that you can refer to it when composing the enlargement.

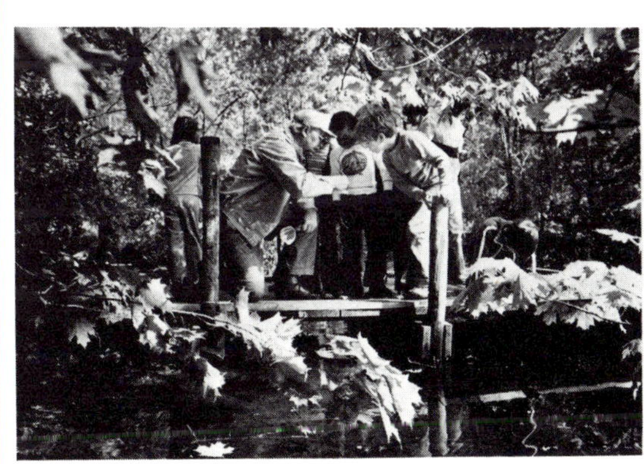

A. Not cropped

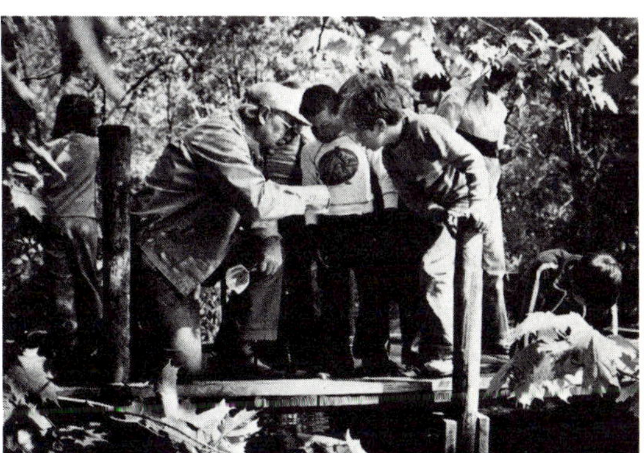

B. Cropped

Fig. 13-1. By cropping, you can omit extra details and emphasize the subject.

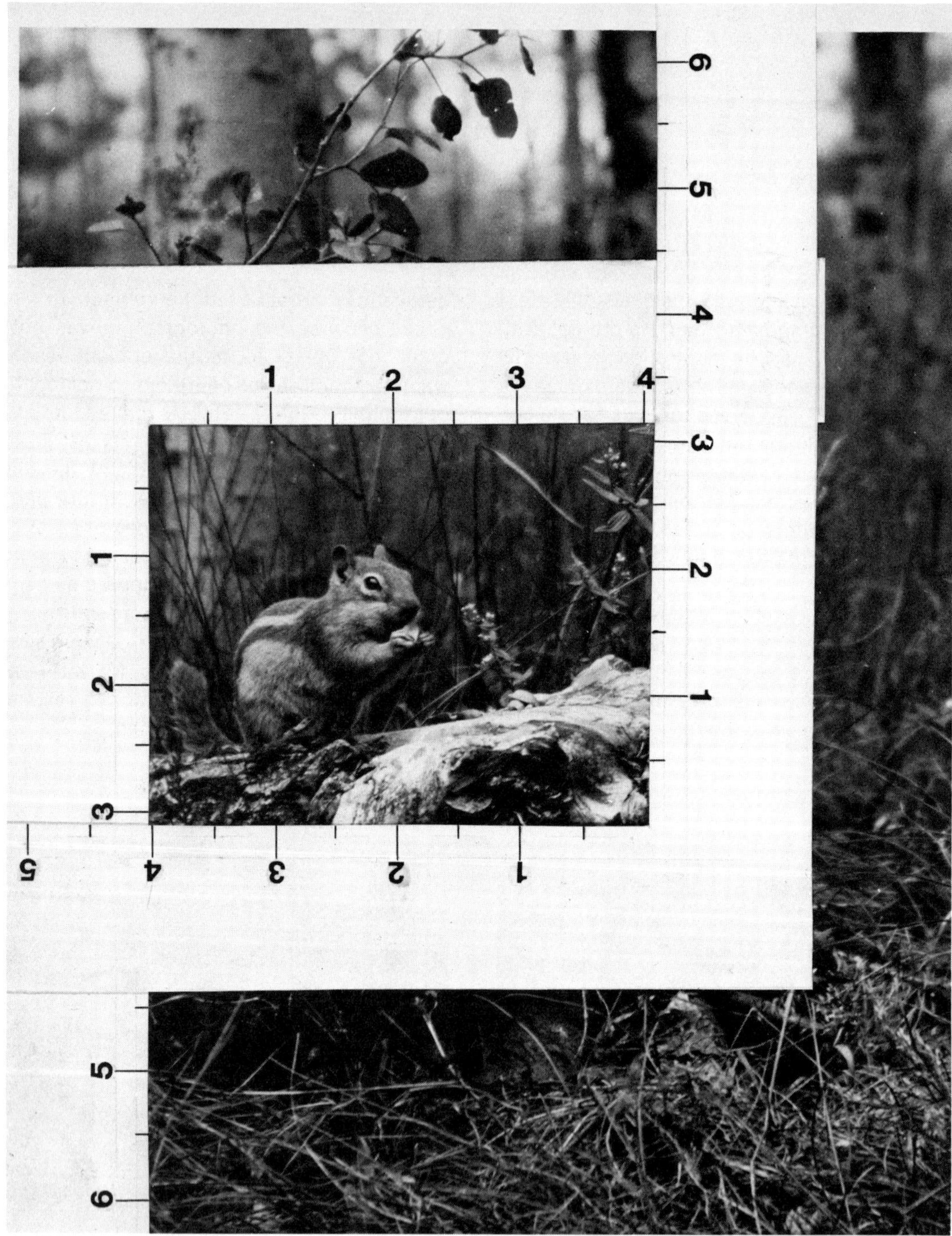

Fig. 13-2. Use two L-shaped pieces of cardboard to find the best part of the picture to keep.

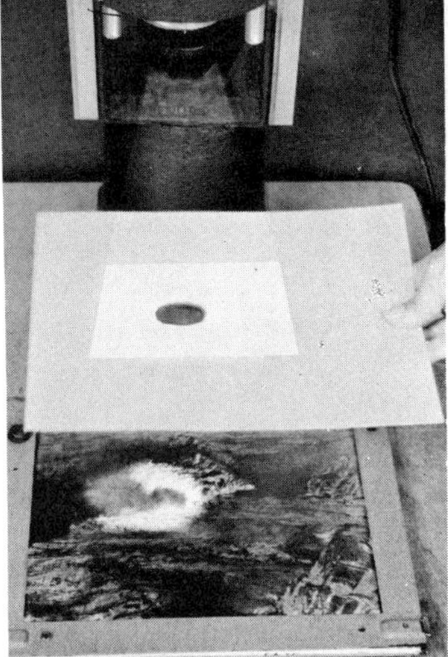

A. Using a device to give added exposure.

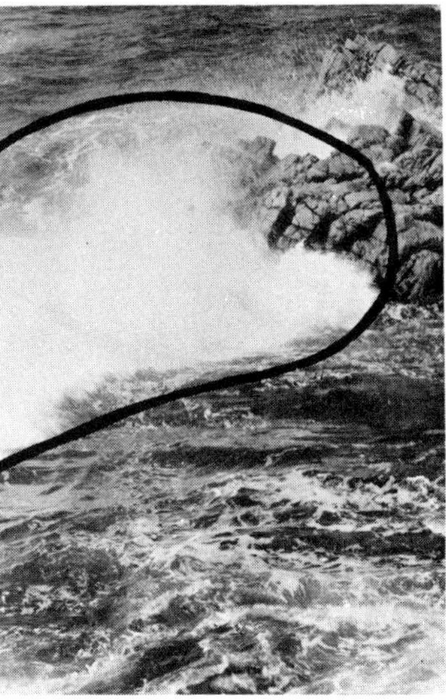

B. Without spot printing.

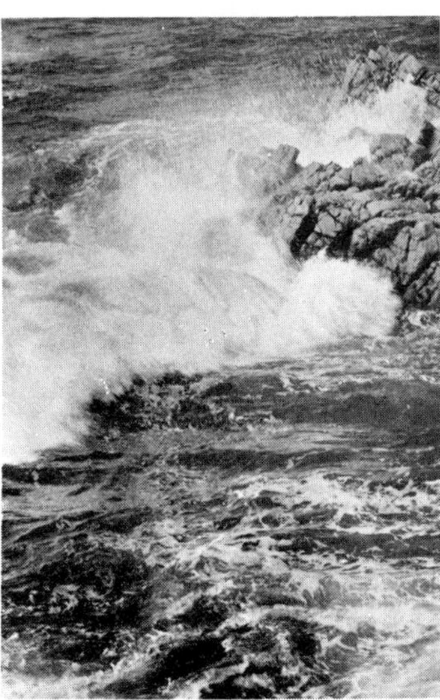

C. With spot printing.

Fig. 13-3. By spot printing, the photographer can develop some light areas, but not overdevelop the entire print.

SPOT PRINTING

Sometimes a small area of a good negative needs more exposure to bring out details. White clouds or ocean waves may need extra exposure to bring out texture and depth. More exposure makes light areas darker, Fig. 13-3. Adding exposure in selected areas is called **spot printing.** The process is also know as **burning in.**

A device is needed that will control the light during exposure. It can be made by cutting a hole in a large piece of cardboard or heavy black paper. The card is held between the lens and the paper as shown in Fig. 13-3. Light allowed to enter the hole is directed to the desired area on the print being made. The large cardboard prevents the remainder of the picture from being further exposed. Keep the cardboard in gentle motion. This blends the edges of the area with the remainder of the picture.

DODGING

When an area in a picture is darker than desired, it can be lightened on a new print by **dodging,** Fig. 13-4. The dark area is **shielded** from light during part of the exposure time. This causes the area to be lighter and to show more details when developed. Dodging is the opposite procedure of burning in. The tool for dodging is a small piece of dark cardboard or paper cut to any desired shape and fastened to a thin stiff wire, Fig. 13-5.

Make a test strip of the print to determine the correct length of exposure. It is helpful to regulate the lens opening so that the exposure time is 30 seconds or more. This gives time to do a better job of dodging where needed.

Hold the dodging tool between the lens and the paper. Keep it in constant motion to blend the edges with the remainder of the picture. Also, be sure to change the position of the

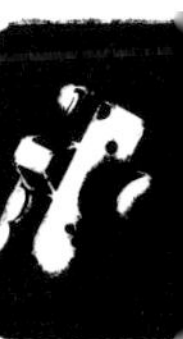

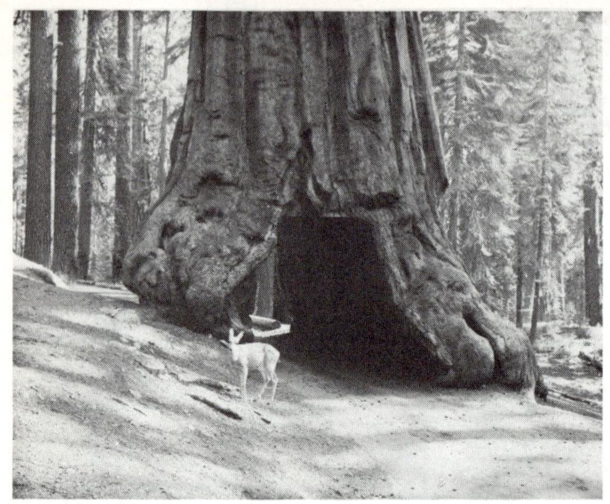

A. Without dodging.

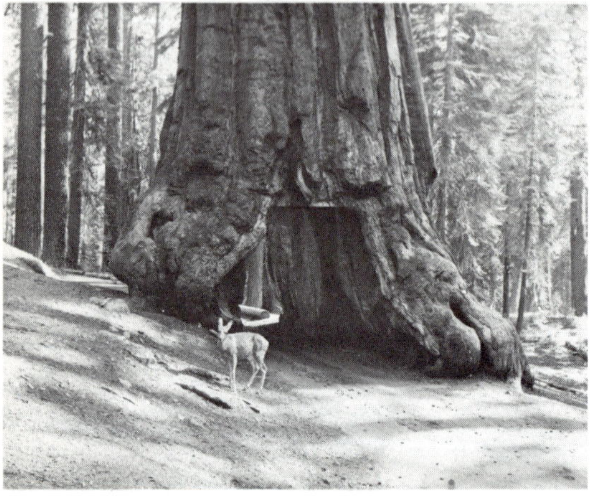

B. With dodging.

Fig. 13-4. Dodging shades an area during exposure so that it does not get too dark. Notice the difference in detail inside the tree.

wire handle so that you do not get a white line on your print caused by the shadow of the wire.

Example:

Close the lens so that the proper time for the most of the print is 40 seconds. Study the test strip to determine the best time for the area to be dodged, in this case 20 seconds. Expose the entire print for 20 seconds. Then slip the dodging tool in place. Keep it in constant rotary

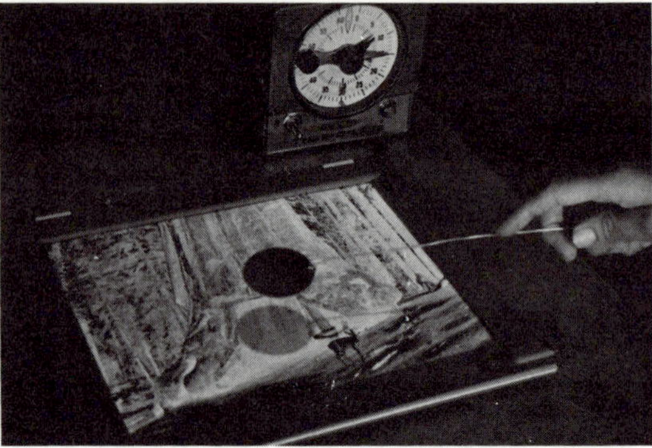

Fig. 13-5. Dodging shades an area of the picture. This allows some dark areas to turn out lighter on the final print.

or vertical motion for the remaining 20 seconds and keep changing the position of the handle.

CORRECTING DISTORTION

Distortion results when the camera must be tilted up or down to take the picture. This often happens when taking pictures of walls, tall buildings, or trees. Their vertical lines seem to converge or move closer at one end. The base of a building, being closer to the lens than the top, looks wider on film than the top of the building. See Fig. 13-6. This is a natural law of perspective. We see things in perspective every day, but our eyes automatically compensate for it. When we see it in a print, this compensation does not occur, and the subject looks distorted.

Sometimes distortion can be corrected when the picture is taken. You can, however, correct some distortion while making the enlargement. The procedure for correcting distortion is as follows:

1. With the negative in the enlarger and a focusing paper in the easel, open the lens to its maximum aperture and turn on the light.
2. Adjust the focus until it is correct.
3. Tilt the easel so that the image of the bottom of the building is closer to the lens than the top of the building, Figure 13-7. The easel is

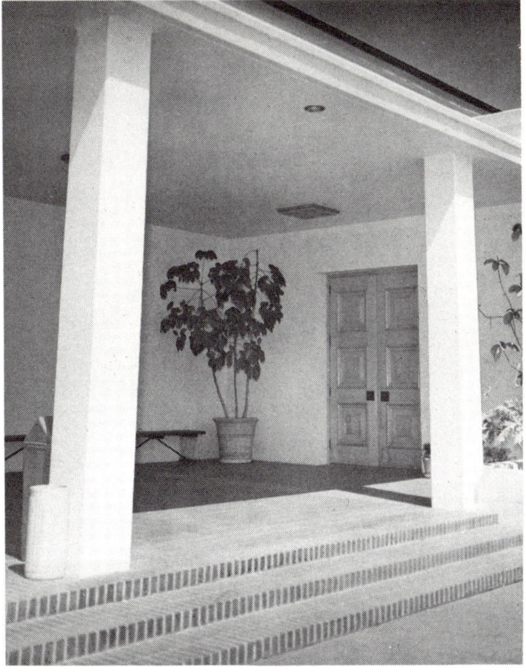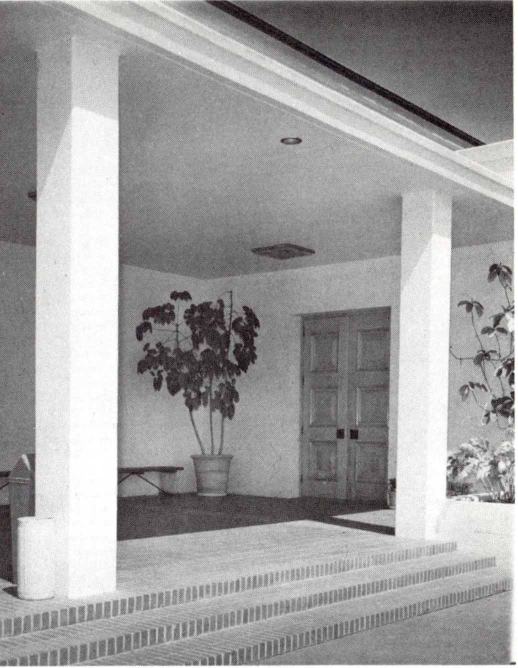

Fig. 13-6. The picture on the left looks distorted due to convergance. On the right, distortion was corrected during printing.

tilted until the lines of the side of the building are parallel to the side of the easel. There is a practical limit. This slant must not be greater than the depth of field.

4. Prop the easel securely in this position.
5. If the enlarger lens can be tilted, tilt the lens so that it is parallel with the easel. If the lens cannot be tilted, choose an object a little above the center and focus critically with the lens wide open.
6. Close the lens to its smaller aperture. This gives maximum depth of field.
7. Make a test strip to determine the correct exposure. This is necessary because, if the easel is greatly tilted, the part farthest away needs more exposure than the part closest to the lens.
8. When exposing the finished print, give the entire print the proper exposure for the part nearest the lens. With a piece of cardboard

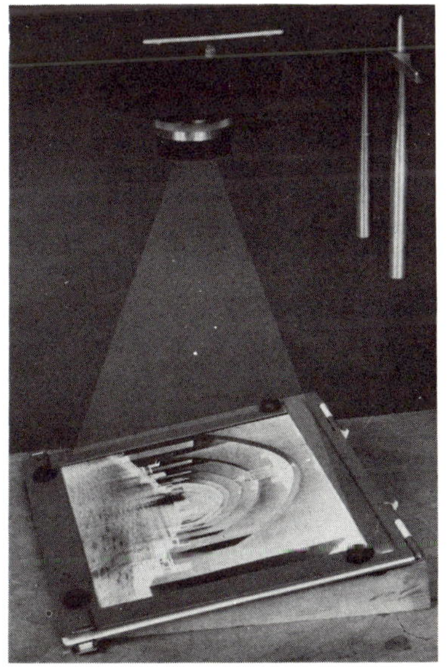
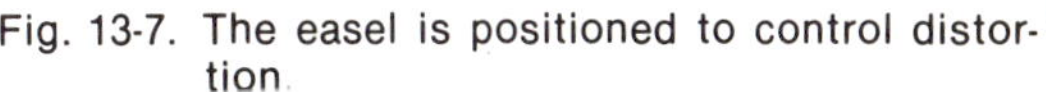
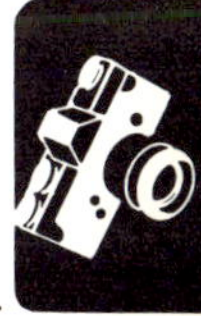

Fig. 13-7. The easel is positioned to control distortion.

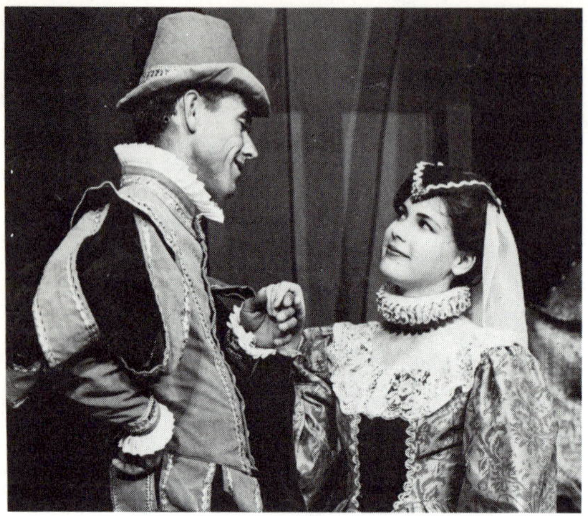

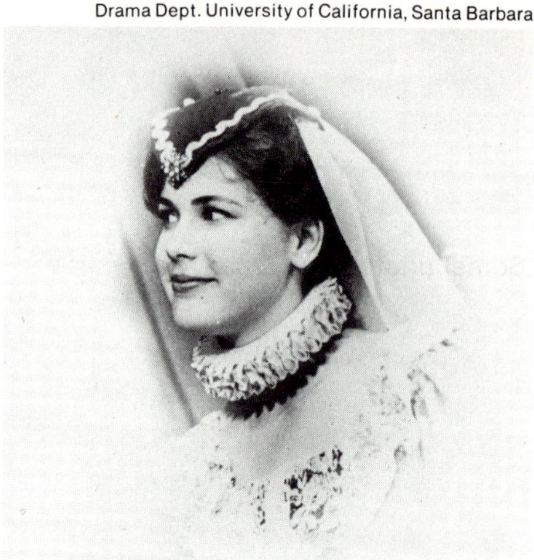

Drama Dept. University of California, Santa Barbara

Fig. 13-8. Vignetting allows you to block out all unwanted areas of the picture. Here a vignette of an actress is made from a photograph taken during a play.

start at the part nearest the lens and gradually shade to the part farthest from the lens. Keep the cardboard in motion at all times. Practice this a few times before exposing the paper so that the rate of moving the cardboard will be correct to give correct exposure to all parts of the print.

VIGNETTING

On occasion, only a small portion of a picture is desired. This is often the case with a picture of a group of people. Sometimes one person may move as the picture is taken and spoil the picture, but another in the group has an especially good picture. An enlargement can be made of this one person of the group by a little trick known as **vignetting,** Fig. 13-8. In this technique, there are no definite borders on the picture. The subject fades gradually into the white paper.

Follow these steps to make a vignette:

1. Cut a hole in cardboard or black paper to match the shape of the image desired, but somewhat smaller.
2. Cut notches all around the hole, Fig. 13-9.

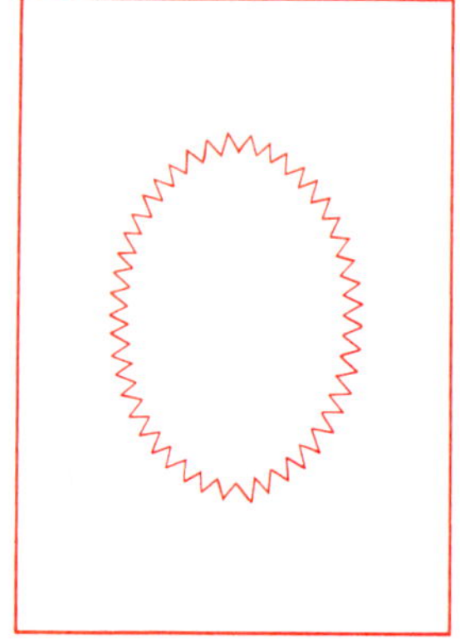

Fig. 13-9. Cardboard mask used for vignetting.

3. Determine the exposure time as described earlier, and place the photo paper in place as for a regular enlargement.
4. Turn on the enlarger so that the image appears on the photo paper. Hold the prepared cardboard part way between the enlarger lens and the paper, adjust its position so that only the image you want can be seen on the paper.

5. Rotate the cardboard gently and move up and down so that the edges fade gradually.
6. Finish the print in the usual manner.

DIFFUSING

Some photographs can be improved by softening sharp details. This process is called **diffusing.** A diffusion disc or plate is placed next to the enlarging lens during the exposure. The disc is a flat piece of glass that scatters the light just enough to break up the sharp edges on the image. Note the effect that results from this technique in Fig. 13-10. One thickness of women's nylon stockings stretched over a frame can be substituted for the diffusion disc.

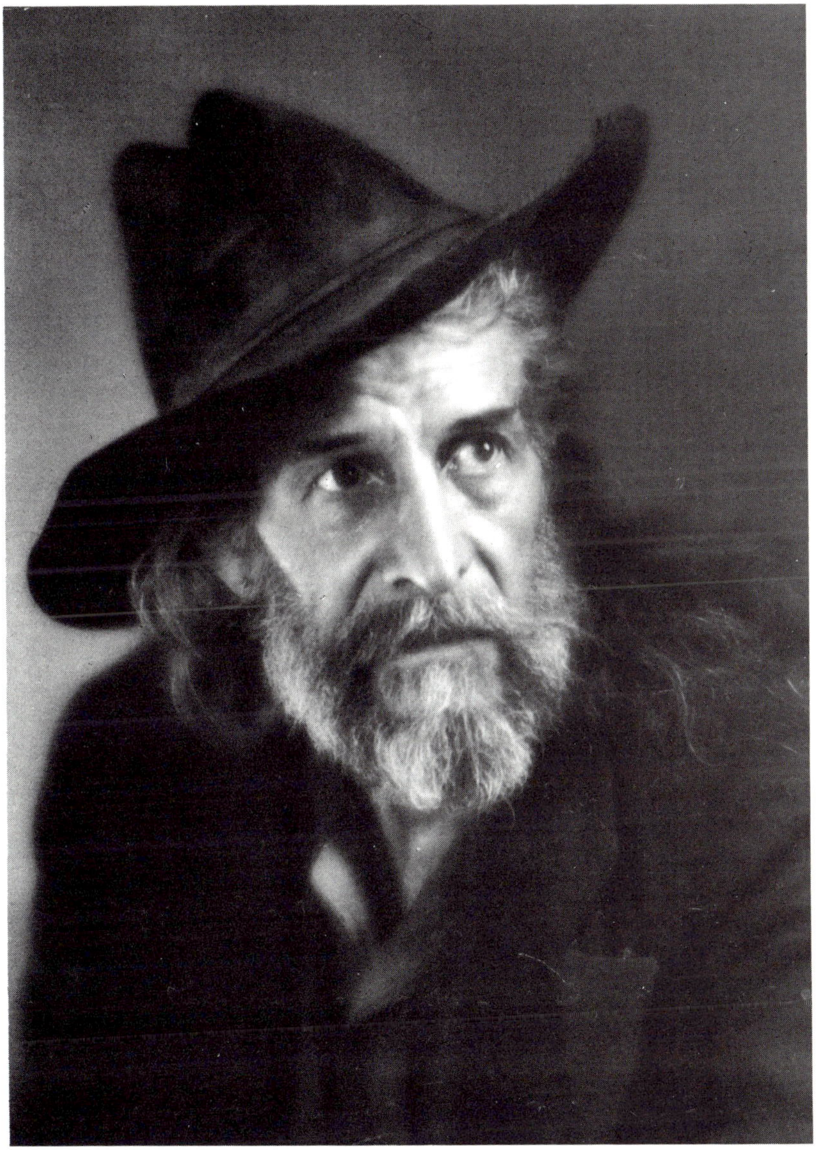

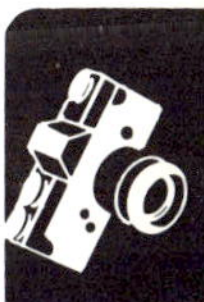

Fig. 13-10. Using a diffusing disk to soften sharp lines makes this portrait more interesting and attractive.

To diffuse a picture, keep the disc moving up and down and around in circles during the exposure. The degree of diffusion is controlled by the amount of time the diffusion disc is used. Try using the diffusion disc for about half of the normal exposure time for your first print. Exposure time must be increased when the diffuser is used. Make a test strip to check both the diffusion and exposure time.

STUDY QUESTIONS

1. Define cropping. When is it used?
2. Explain spot printing. When would you use this technique?
3. Explain dodging. When would you use this technique?
4. How can you correct distortion when making an enlargement?
5. Describe the vignetting technique and give an instance for use.
6. What effect does diffusing give to an enlargement?

ACTIVITY 13 — USING ADVANCED DARKROOM PROCEDURES

Assignment

Choose at least two printing techniques listed under "Procedure". Prepare to hand in the negatives, prints, and any device required in the techniques you choose.

Materials Needed

4 to 10 sheets 5 x 7 in. polycontrast F paper
Darkroom supplies

Procedure

Complete at least two of the following assignments.

1. Cropping for proper composition
   a. Choose a negative.
   b. Make a 5 x 7 in. uncropped print.
   c. Make a final 5 x 7 in. cropped print.
   d. Hand in both prints and your negative.
2. Spot Printing
   a. Choose a negative with areas that need spot printing. (Your teacher may have to help you choose.)
   b. Make a 5 x 7 in. untreated print.
   c. Make a 5 x 7 in. print improved by spot printing.
   d. Hand in both prints and your negative.
3. Dodging
   Repeat the same procedure as for spot printing, choosing a negative having an area that can be improved by dodging.
4. Vignetting
   a. Choose a negative which has a subject you wish to emphasize.
   b. Make a regular 5 x 7 in. print of the negative.
   c. Make a vignetting mask. Remember that it should be slightly smaller than the area you wish to print.
   d. Make a vignetted print.
   e. Hand in your prints, negative and vignetting mask.
5. Diffusing
   a. Choose a clear sharp negative that could be improved by diffusing.
   b. Make a regular 5 x 7 in. print. Do not diffuse.
   c. Make a 5 x 7 in. print using a diffusing disc or nylon stocking.
   d. Hand in both prints, your negative, and diffusing device if you made one. Also, hand in a record of how long you used the diffusing disc.
6. Distortion Correction (optional)
   See your teacher for a negative having a distorted subject.

Chapter **14**   **BUYING FILM AND LENSES**

FILM

Most camera stores carry a wide selection of types and brands of film. The amateur photographer can be confused about which film to buy. However, the choice is not as complicated as it seems. You should consider two main points when buying film:

1. Do you want slides, black and white prints, or color prints?
2. Where and when will you be taking the pictures?

The choice of slides or prints is a personal one. It depends upon what you are going to do with the pictures. Prints are best to put in albums or send to family and friends. Slides are generally preferred for scenery. Also, you can share your pictures on slides with large groups of people.

Black and white film is less expensive to process. For many purposes it is just as good, if not better, than color. Color film, on the other hand, is more realistic. It is often preferred for snapshots of family and friends.

FILM ASA

The ASA rating, as you know, shows the film's sensitivity to light. The initials ASA stand for American Standards Association, the agency that made the ratings. (This agency is now called the American National Standards Institute.)

Film ASA is the main consideration in choosing black and white film. Films having an ASA of 50 or less are considered slow films. Medium speed films have an ASA of around 100. Fast films are an ASA of 250 or more. The **ASA number doubles** each time the speed of the **film doubles.** If a film has an ASA rating of 250, it is twice as fast as an ASA 125 film. The ASA 250 film needs only half the light exposure than the slower ASA 125 film does to make a negative of the same density. Fast film allows the photographer to shoot at a faster shutter speed. A small aperture can be used to increase the depth of field. Also, fast films are used for shooting in low light conditions without a flash, Fig. 14-1.

Fast films have one disadvantage. They tend to produce grainier pictures. In theory, you should use the slowest film possible in each situation. However, this can pose problems for the amateur photographer. Generally, a medium or fast film gives good results in most situations.

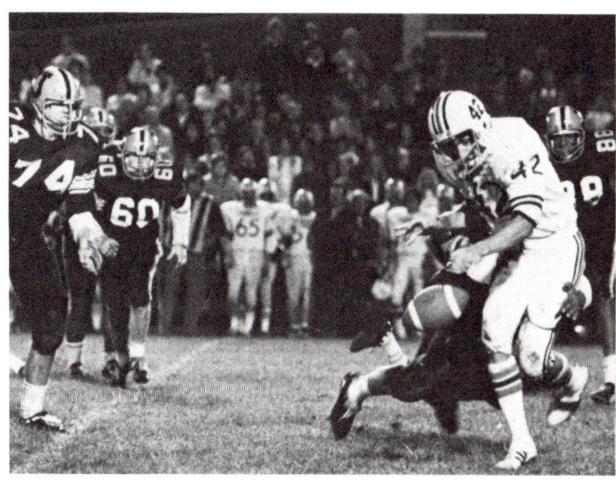

Fig. 14-1. Fast film allows the photographer to use a fast shutter speed, shoot in low light, or increase the depth of field.

COLOR FILM

Color film selection requires that you identify the setting in which it will be used. This includes whether the pictures will be taken outdoors, indoors with natural lighting, or indoors with artificial lighting. Outdoor film used indoors may change the colors unless flash lighting is used. If artificial lighting is used indoors, it may be photoflood of the tungsten type, photoflood of the quartz type, electronic flash, or blue flashcubes. Each of these will affect the choice of film.

Another factor in choosing color film is the desired amount of detail sharpness. The speed of the film affects the grain of the picture. Slow films show sharp detail. Fast films lack this sharpness and are more grainy. However, fast films are selected for difficult lighting situations and action pictures.

Color films vary in overall color quality. Films are produced to have emulsions sensitive to colors on a scale of cool colors (blue) to warm colors (reds). The choice of film depends on the desired end result. Some color films tend to intensify certain colors. This gives the picture colors that appear stronger than the un-aided eye records. Amateur photographers may want to ask their photographic supplier for help in choosing color film.

GENERAL NOTES

The size film you buy depends upon the camera you are using. Choose the correct size for your type of camera. When you buy film, check the expiration date on the side of the film package. Slightly outdated film will still give

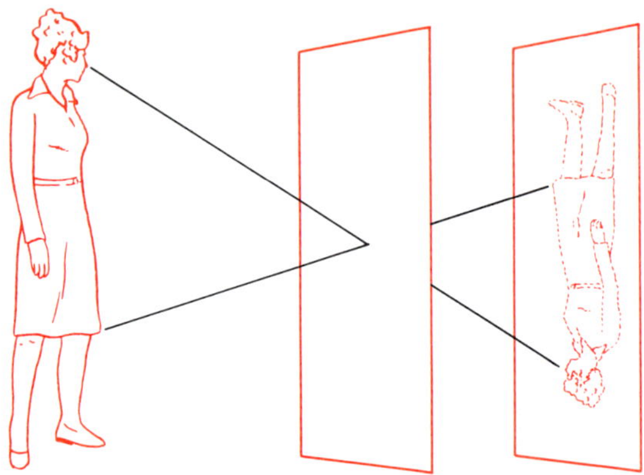

Fig. 14-3. A pinhole can organize light rays because only a few from each point can get through the pinhole. If the pinhole were bigger, the rays would scatter and not form an image.

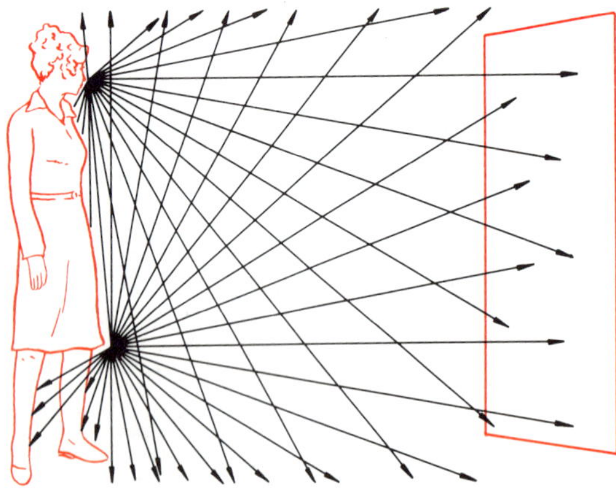

Fig. 14-2. Uncontrolled light rays, shown reflected from two points—the face and dress—travel in all directions. They will not form an image on the film.

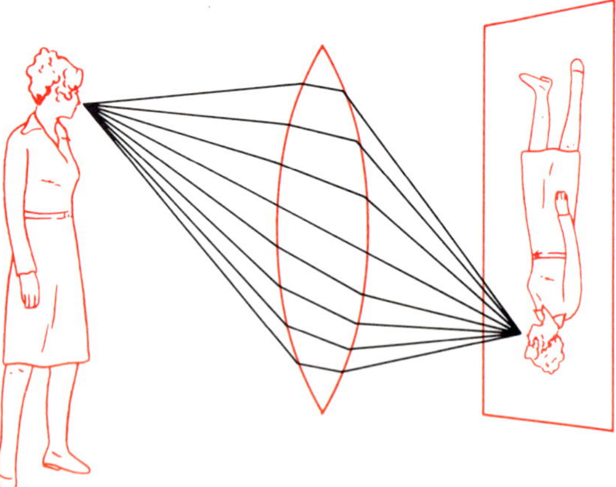

Fig. 14-4. The purpose of a lens is to organize the light rays so that they form a clear image on the film.

good results if it has been stored properly. However, after the expiration date a loss of speed and quality begins to occur.

How you store your film is important. Heat can destroy film, so do not leave it in a hot car or near a stove. Film keeps well in the refrigerator or freezer as long as it is in moisture-proof wrapping. Before you unwrap refrigerated film, let it warm up to room temperature so that water does not condense on the surface.

Load and unload your camera out of strong light. Put exposed film back in its protective wrapping and develop the film within a few days after it has been exposed.

If you have any questions concerning film or your camera, ask a reputable photo dealer. Often dealers are experienced photographers who are glad to pass along their know-how to beginners.

LENSES

Before a camera can form an image on film, the light entering must be shaped and controlled. You cannot simply place film in front of a subject and expect to get a picture, Fig. 14-2. The rays reflecting off the subject would hit the film in a random mass. Although Fig. 14-2 shows light reflecting off two points of the subject, all points of the subject reflect rays. A light control device is needed in front of the film that will organize the rays so that a clear picture results. A lens controls the light rays. All lenses work in the same basic way. They collect the light rays and project them onto the film. Figures 14-3 and 14-4 show how a pinhole and a lens organize the rays.

Different types of lenses can be used on many cameras. The photographer must know which one to use to get the picture desired. Mainly, lenses differ in their focal length. **Focal length** is the distance from the lens to a point behind the lens where the light rays are focused when the distance scale is set on infinity. The main thing to remember is that as the focal length of the lens gets shorter, the size of the subject becomes smaller, but the view becomes wider. In Fig. 14-5, notice that the subject is smaller when the 28 mm lens is used than when the 50 mm lens is used.

The diagram in Fig. 14-6 shows the differences in the focal length of 28 mm, 50 mm, 135 mm, 300 mm, and 500 mm lenses. As you can see, the size of the image increases in proportion to the focal length. The 28 mm, having a short focal length, takes the **widest** angle, but the image is the smallest. As the focal length gets longer with each larger lens, the angle gets

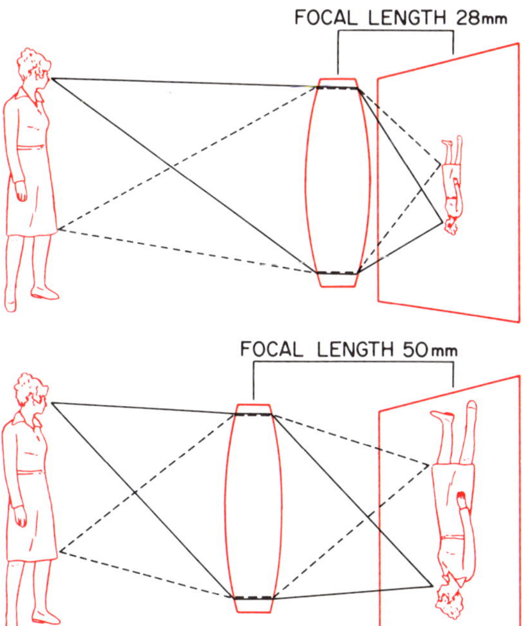

Fig. 14-5. The focal length of the lens determines the angle of view and how much the subject is magnified. Notice how much the size of the image changes when the 28 mm and 50 mm lenses are used.

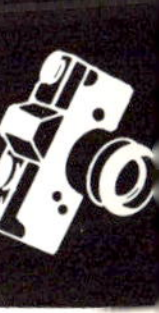

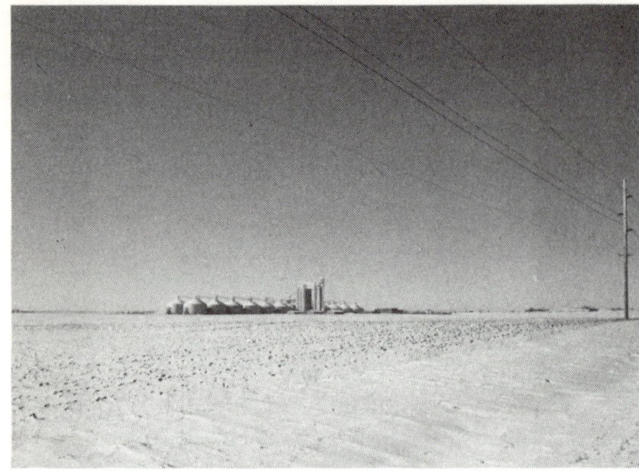

A. 28 mm

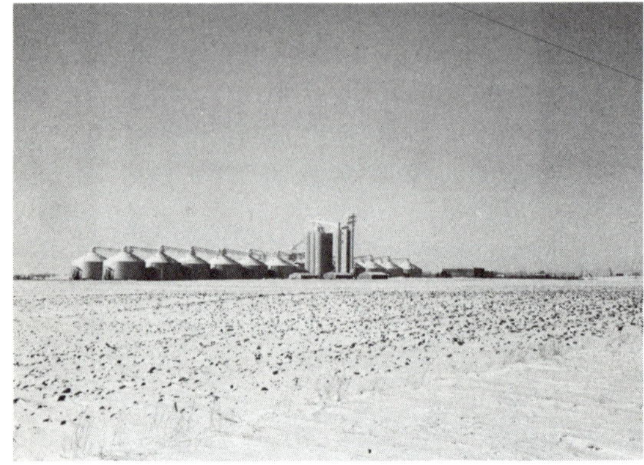

B. 50 mm

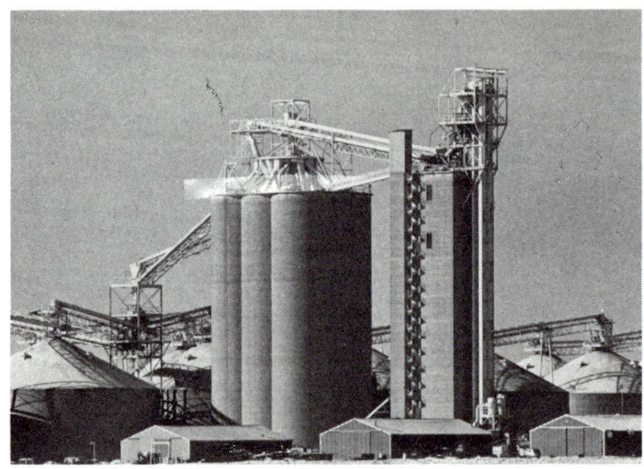

C. 135 mm

D. 300 mm

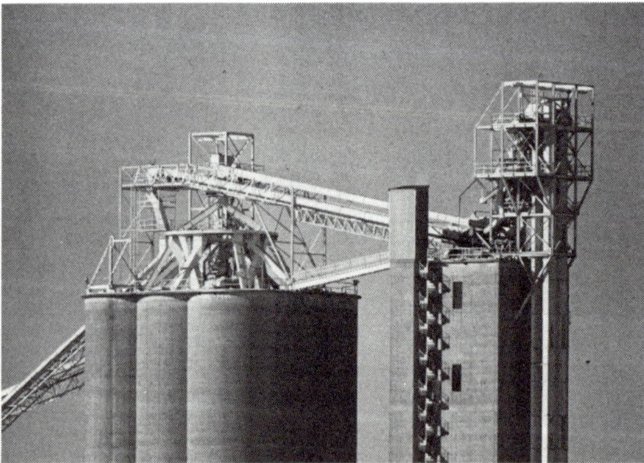

E. 500 mm

Fig. 14-6. Focal length controls the size of the image formed by the lens and the angle of view—that is, the amount of the scene included in the image on film. The size of the image increases in proportion to the focal length.

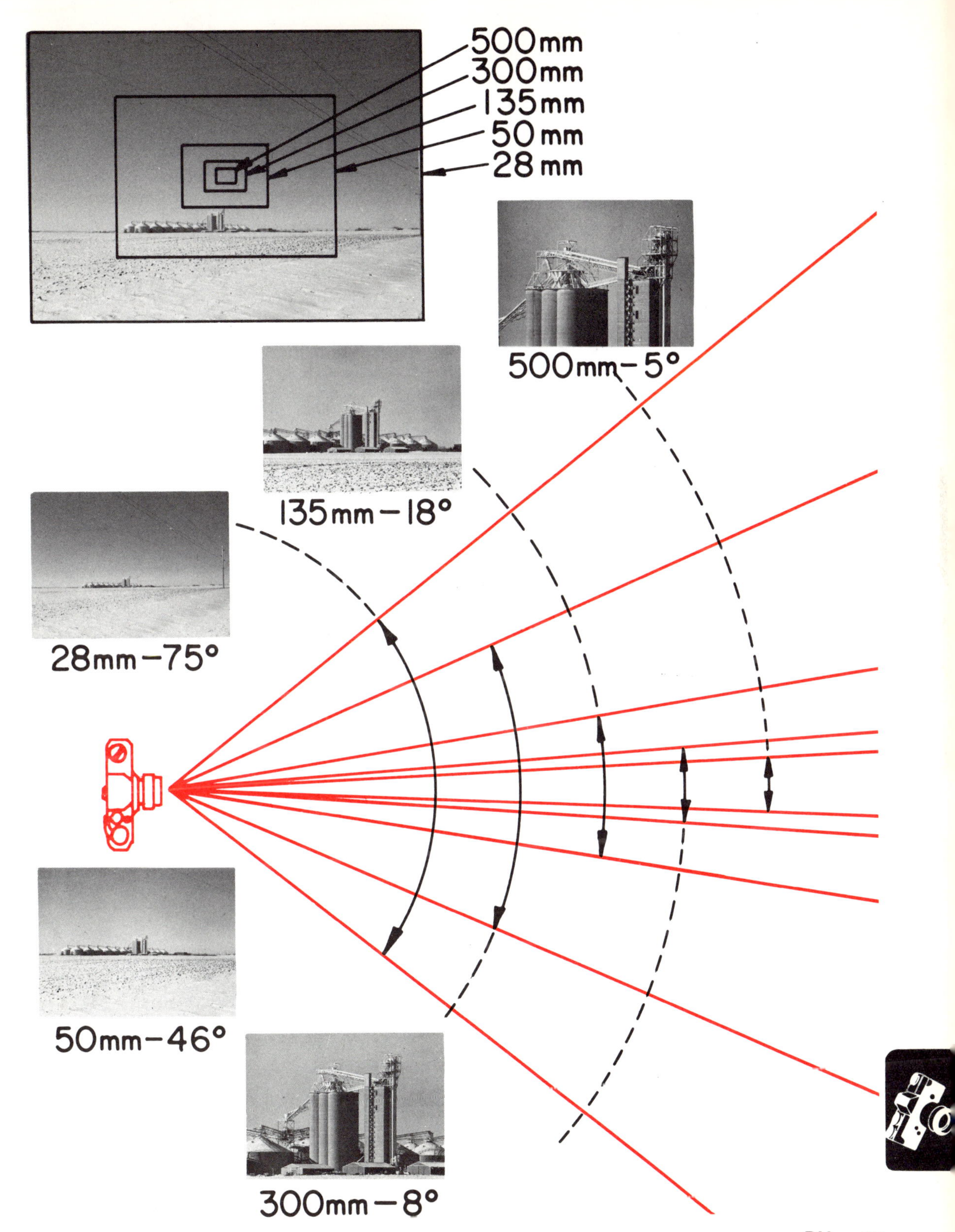

500mm—5°

135mm—18°

28mm—75°

50mm—46°

300mm—8°

narrower, but the image gets bigger. A lens that magnifies the image, such as the 300 and 500 mm lenses, is called a **telephoto lens.** The reason a telephoto lens has such a small angle of view can be shown by this simple experiment. Make a circle with your thumb and forefinger and hold it close to your eye. You wil see most of the scene. Now, continue to look through the circle as you move it away from your eye. The circle will be filled by a smaller part of the scene. You have decreased the angle of view. Telephoto lenses work on the same principle.

STUDY QUESTIONS

1. What is ASA? If you were taking action shots or shooting in low light, would you buy a film with a low or high ASA rating?
2. What is meant by a slow film? What is the advantage of slow films over fast films?
3. How should you store your film?
4. What happens to film that is outdated?
5. What is the purpose of a lens?
6. Explain what happens to magnification and angle of view when you use a lens having a long focal length (telephoto lens).

A GLOSSARY OF PHOTOGRAPHIC TERMS

Action shot — The subject is moving while the picture is being taken.

Adjustable camera — A camera on which distance settings, lens openings, and shutter speeds are adjusted by hand.

Adjustable-focus lens — A lens that can be adjusted for distance.

Agitate — Gently keeping the developer, stop bath, or fixer in motion while processing film or paper. This helps to ensure even development and prevent spotting or staining.

Angle of view — The part of a scene that is seen by a camera lens. The width of this wedge-shaped portion is determined by the focal length of the lens. A wide-angle lens having short focal length includes a wider angle of view than a normal lens having normal focal length or a telephoto lens having long focal length.

Aperture — The opening in the diaphragm through which light passes. Aperture size may be fixed or adjustable. F-stops determine the size of the diaphragm opening.

ASA — A rating that describes the sensitivity of the film to light. The ASA rating doubles as the sensitivity of the film doubles. A film with a high ASA rating is called a fast film.

Automatic camera — One with a built-in exposure meter that automatically sets the lens opening, shutter speed, or both, for proper exposure.

Background — The part of the picture that is behind the subject.

Back lighting — Light shining on the subject from the opposite direction of camera. Distinguished from front lighting and side lighting.

Balance — Placement of colors, light and dark masses, or large and small objects in a picture to create harmony. An element of composition.

Blowup — An enlargement. A print made bigger than the negative or slide.

Bounce light — Light that does not travel directly to the subject from the flash, but is reflected off another surface.

Burning in — Giving extra exposure to part of the image projected on an enlarger easel to make that area of the print darker. This is done after the basic exposure by lengthening the exposure time to let more light strike the areas in the print you want to darken while holding back the light from the rest of the image. Sometimes called spot printing.

Camera angles — Different positions of the camera (high, medium, or low; and left, right, or straight on) with respect to the subject. Each angle gives a different viewpoint or effect.

Candid pictures — Unposed pictures, often taken without the subject's knowledge. These usually appear more natural and relaxed than posed pictures.

Carrier — A frame that holds a negative in the enlarger. Also called a negative holder.

Clearing agent — A chemical that neutralizes hypo on film or paper. It reduces washing time and helps to provide a more stable image.

Closeup — A picture taken with the camera close to the subject.

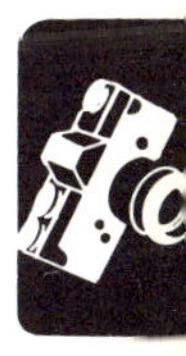

Closeup lens — A lens attachment placed in front of a camera lens to permit taking pictures at a closer distance than the camera lens alone would allow.

Composition — The arrangement of all parts of a picture — main subject, foreground, and supporting subjects.

Contact print — One made by placing the negative against photographic paper. Images in the print will be the same size as those in the negative.

Contrast — The density range of a negative, print, or slide. The brightness range of a subject or the scene lighting.

Contrasty — Too high in contrast. The range of density in a negative or print is too great.

Cropping — Using only part of the picture that is in the negative or slide.

Darkroom — A light-tight room used for processing films and for printing and processing papers. Also used for loading and unloading some cameras.

Daylight film — Color film that is designed for use in natural sunlight. Daylight film indoors with regular lights will have a yellowish cast. This can be corrected with a filter.

Density — The blackness of an area in a negative or print which determines the amount of light that will pass through it or reflect from it.

Depth of field — The distance range between the nearest and farthest objects that appear in focus in a photograph. It depends on the f-stop, the focal length of the lens, and the distance from the lens to the subject.

Developer — A solution used to make the image visible on exposed films or photographic papers.

Developing tank — A light-tight container used for processing film.

Diaphragm — An adjustable opening mounted behind or between the elements of a lens. It is used to control the amount of light that reaches the film. Openings are usually measured in f-stops.

Dodging — Holding back the light from a part of the image projected on an enlarger easel during part of the basic exposure time. Used to make the area of the print lighter.

Double exposure — Two pictures taken on one frame of film, or two images printed on one piece of photographic paper.

Electronic flash — A reusable flash device. It is sometimes called a strobe.

Emulsion — A thin coating of light-sensitive material, usually silver halide in gelatin. The image is formed on film and photographic papers by the emulsion.

Emulsion side — The side of the film coated with emulsion. In contact printing and enlarging, the emulsion side is the dull side of the photographic paper.

Enlargement — A print that is larger than the negative or slide. Sometimes called a blowup.

Enlarger — A device having a light source, a negative holder, a lens, and a means of adjusting these to project an enlarged image from a negative onto a sheet of photographic paper.

Exposure — The amount of light allowed to reach the film or to act on a photographic paper. A product of the intensity (controlled by the shutter speed or enlarging time) of light striking the film or paper.

Exposure setting — The lens opening and shutter speed selected to expose the film.

Fast — (1) A film or paper that is very sensitive to light. (2) A lens that opens to a very wide aperture. (3) A short shutter speed. The opposite of slow.

Film speed — The sensitivity of a given film to light, indicated by a ASA number. The higher the number, the more sensitive or "faster" the film.

Fixed-focus lens — A lens that has been focused in a fixed position by the manufacturer. The user does not have to adjust the focus of this type of lens.

Fixer — A solution that removes any light-sensitive crystals not acted upon by light or developer.

Flash — A brief, intense burst of light produced by a flashbulb or an electronic flash unit, usually used when there is not enough light for picture taking.

Flat — Too low in contrast. The range in density in a negative or print is too short.

F-stop — A number on most adjustable cameras used to indicate the size and light-passing ability of the lens opening. Common f-stops are f/2.8, f/4, f/5.6, f/8, f/11, f/16, and f/22. The larger the f-number, the smaller the lens opening. In this series, f/2.8 is the largest lens opening and f/22 is smallest lens opening.

Focal length — The distance from the lens to a point behind the lens where light rays are focused when the distance scale is set on infinity. Focal length determines the size of the image at a given lens-to-subject distance.

Focus — Adjustment of the distance setting on a lens so that the subject is sharply defined.

Foreground — The area between the camera and the principal subject.

Front lighting — Light shining on the subject from the direction of the camera.

Glossy — A shiny printing paper. The opposite of matte.

Graininess — The sand-like or granular appearance of a negative, print, or slide resulting from the clumping of silver crystals during development of the film. Graininess is noticed more with faster films, increased density in the negative, and degree of enlargement.

Guide number — A number used to determine the f-stop needed to expose film with a flash. The number varies with the ASA of the film and the power of the flash. To figure exposure, divide the guide number by the distance from the camera to the subject.

High contrast — A wide range of density in a print or negative. Big difference between light and dark areas.

Highlights — The brightest areas of a subject and the areas in a negative, print, or slide.

Hypo — The name for a fixing bath made from sodium thiosulfate, other chemicals, and water. Often called a fixing bath.

Interchangeable lens — A lens that can be removed from the camera and replaced with another lens, usually of a different focal length.

Lens — One or more pieces of optical glass or similar material designed to collect and focus rays of light to form a sharp image on the film, paper, or projection screen.

Lens speed — The largest lens opening (smallest f-stop) at which a lens can be set. A "fast" lens transmits more light and has a larger opening than a "slow" lens.

Lighting — The light falling on a subject. Also the direction or arrangement of light. Back, front, and side are the common sources of lighting.

Long shot — A scene taken from a relatively long distance. The main subject usually appears quite small in respect to the entire frame size.

Medium shot — A picture made about halfway between a long and closeup shot to appear as the normal viewing distance.

Negative — The developed film that contains a reversed image of the original scene.

Negative holder — A device that holds the negative in proper position in an enlarger. Also called a carrier.

Normal lens — A lens that makes the image in a photograph appear in a perspective similar to that of the original scene. A normal lens has a shorter focal length and a wider field of view than a telephoto lens and a longer focal length and narrower field of view than a wide-angle lens.

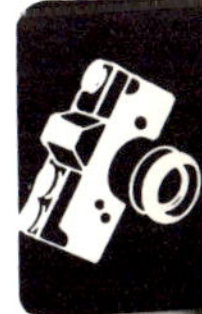

Notching code — Notches cut in the margin of sheet film so that the type of film and its emulsion side can be identified in the dark.

One-shot developer — A developing solution that is used just once, then thrown away.

Open up — To increase the size of the lens aperture. The opposite of stop down.

Overexposure — A condition in which too much light reaches the film. It produces a dense negative or a washed-out print or slide.

Panning — Moving the camera along with a moving subject. The subject will be sharp and the background blurred.

Perspective — The assumed size and distance of objects in a picture.

Photogram — An image made by placing an object on photographic paper, then exposing it to light.

Positive — The opposite of a negative. An image with the same color relationships as those in the original scene. For example, a finished print or a slide.

Print — A positive picture, usually on paper, and usually produced from a negative.

Printing frame — A device used for contact printing that holds a negative against the photographic paper. The paper is exposed by light from an external light source.

Roll film — Film that comes in rolls, rather than sheets. Roll film is usually packaged in cartridges or cassettes.

Safelight — An enclosed darkroom lamp fitted with a filter to screen out light rays to which film and paper are sensitive.

Sharp — An image or part of an image that shows crisp, precise texture and detail. The opposite of blurred or soft.

Sheet film — Film that is cut into individual flat pieces. Also called cut film.

Shutter — A device in the camera which controls the time during which light reaches the film.

Sidelighting — Light striking the subject from the side relative to the position of the camera. It produces shadows and highlights on the subject.

Silver halide — The light sensitive crystals in the film emulsion.

Slide — A photographic transparency, usually color, mounted for projection.

Slow — See fast.

Speed — (1) The relative sensitivity of film and paper to light. (2) The relative ability of a lens to let in more light by opening to a wider aperture.

Stop — (1) A diaphragm setting determining the aperture (f-stop). (2) A change in exposure by a factor of two. One more f-stop doubles the light reaching the film or paper. One stop less cuts the amount of light in half. (3) Stop bath see below.

Stop bath — An acid rinse, usually a weak solution of acetic acid, used as a second step when developing black-and-white film or paper. It stops development and makes the hypo last longer.

Stop down — To decrease the size of the lens aperture. Opposite: open up.

Synchronize — To make the flash go off at the same time that the shutter is open.

Telephoto lens — A lens that makes a subject appear larger on film than a normal lens does at the same camera-to-subject distance. A telephoto lens has a longer focal length and narrower field of view than a normal lens.

Underexposure — A condition in which too little light reaches the film. It produces a thin negative, dark slide, or muddy-looking print.

Vignetting — Printing the central area of a picture while shading the edges gradually into white.

Wide-angle lens — A lens that has a shorter length and a wider field of view (includes more subject area) than a normal lens.

INDEX

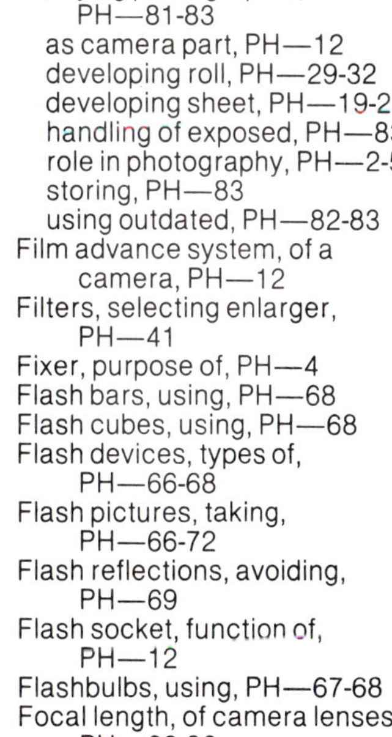

*See the Glossary on pages 87-90 for an alphabetical listing of words with definitions.